Are You Ready For Your Inspection?

VANESSA DOOLEY

VANESSA DOOLEY

DEDICATION

This book is dedicated to all those people who are aiming to make a difference in children's lives. Hoping this will give you some further guidance on improving outcomes for children and making IMPACT.

Remember YOU ARE THE SOURCE

Table of Contents

ACKNOWLEDGEMENTS

Firstly, I have to start by thanking Mr D, my husband for being my critical friend, who has always challenged me to ask myself the question WHY? You were always there to encourage and be the rock and stability in the whole writing process as well as over the past 8 years. My world is a better place with you in it. (Slush moment over!)

My children, Emily and Harry, who I need them to, know how proud I am of what they have achieved. The journey we have travelled over the past 8 years has shown they are resilient, strong and beautiful people. You can achieve anything once you put your mind to it. Go and make a difference.

My parents, aka Terry and Joan.....well what can I say? You are my world and I love you both dearly. The role of daughter to parent is changing in our relationship, but this comes with laughter and tears. Just thank you for making me who I am!

There are many other people who in my life and through the whole writing process have helped me along the way, from Abigail Horne and Sarah Stone from Female Success Network and Authors & Co for giving me the push to excel myself and make my dream a reality. The best decision I ever made was to let you into my creation and help me succeed. Thank you ladies for helping me put the blinkers on.

Thank you to the lovely settings and people who were happy for me to share some of their OUTSTANDING report with others. You really do know how to show IMPACT and are improving outcomes for children. Well done, it's not an easy accomplishment to achieve outstanding.

And finally, but not least, to those cheerleaders in my life who are constantly putting my crown back on straight when crooked without me knowing. Emma Smith (aka Topanga Smith), Amanda Prentice and Carly Craig …You are just the best. You are the most supportive bunch of people I know and I am so honoured to have you in my life. You are constantly chanting encouragement from the side lines alongside shaking your pom poms!

Everyone needs a cheerleader or three in their lives. Find your tribe!

1.THE WHY!

I have often wondered as to why people would want to write books never mind actually going ahead and doing it. I would often be in awe of them for having so much information in their heads that they wanted to get it on paper to share with others. I was also in awe of the fact they were so knowledgeable and brainy to be classified as an author.

Yes, they are good at what they write.

But this attribute alone does not make people brainy; it however, does make them talented in wanting to share what they know.

So when the discussion came throughout my time as a trainer and consultant about why do I not write a book, my first thoughts were a combination of the following -

I do not have that much information in my head to write about.

Do I have the knowledge in the first place?
Another one was…..Who, me? The person who left school with only CSE's …yes, I am that old!

…But then, when I started putting pen to paper, it was more of a mind explosion on paper that I could not seem to stop.

As a friend once said to me… it is like you have brain dumps all that you know on paper.

They were so right.

So, once the brain dump exploded, I needed to put these miniscule pieces of information to create massive pieces of knowledge that would hopefully be of some use.

I became excited and thought WOW…..all this information was actually inside my head, it needed to be released …not only for my sake, but also for others.

This could help people who are in the situation I have been in many times

So now is the time for me to share what I know from both sides of the coin so to speak.

Background

I have always been into early years. As a matter of fact, my passion is Early Years... when Princess Diana announced her engagement to Prince Charles, that's when I knew I wanted to be a nanny. It was the craze...not sure why I wanted to follow in her first steps, but it was indeed massive for to know that actually, there is a job out there that would fit perfectly into my whole perception of meaningful existence. Nowadays, I think I was very lucky to have that thought process very early on... I mean, how many teenagers know what they want to do with their lives when they are at school and take that on?

The thought of achieving the coveted NNEB was beyond my belief, beyond anything I thought I could achieve in my life. Yet, with the help of amazing friends, supportive husband, children and parents and the most inspiring Mrs Espezel (yes we used to call them Mrs in those days), I was able to achieve my ultimate goal.

To cut a long story short, this is where I am today.

I have managed several nurseries and group managed six at one time... that was a huge role for me and one I am so proud of, as it helped me get to where I am today. Without the support of the company owners, I would never have achieved my degree or EYPS; yet another wow moment... putting that gown on, making my parents *and* children proud was just an extraordinarily awesome day.

Leaving the group of nurseries was the hardest thing I've ever had to do, but thinking back to that time now, it was the making of the real me... I've always been determined and passionate. I've had this keen desire to see what else was out there... so I dipped my toes into new pastures and worked my way as an assessor, internal verifier, lecturer, course director for level 2 and 3 as well as the foundation degree...alongside being an Early Years inspector.

Little old me... An inspector and I still pinch myself now thinking how on earth I got that far. But with the most amazing support from my shadow inspector who I still meet for coffee and cake, I did manage to achieve the pinnacle of my career...

But then things started to change... throughout my time in inspecting, I was always asking the question about training and how settings accessed it, how they self-evaluated their practice...staff were petrified when I turned up to inspect, even though throughout the initial phone call, I would try to make them feel at ease... I vividly remembered what it was like... those sick feelings of what I am going to be asked, how the staff will react to the observations being done on them...what if we have got something wrong, and so on.

One thing I do want to say at this stage is that my husband ALWAYS wished me good luck before I left the house before an inspection. Why do you ask? Because as an inspector, you are entering someone else's domain, home, pride and joy; you are on your own... so think about that when you ask your inspector in...

So anyway, throughout the inspections, I realised that I needed to get the best out of the setting and the staff. Inevitably, the only way to do that was for them to feel confident in their own setting and shine... yes...SHINE

This is your one and only chance to show how good you really are. This is your chance to ensure all the needs of your children, staff and your own self are being met whilst ascertaining the level of impact you are making.

The word IMPACT will be a common theme in this book alongside SO WHAT!

When doing my inspector training, the senior inspection drilled it into us when we were writing our report - SO WHAT - and I have taken this throughout my consultancy and training... in fact so much so that I am now seeing those words being used in settings when I revisit them.

So this is where this book comes into its own. I wanted to share with you, help you feel empowered and get prepared for your inspection.

There is no manual on this critical element.

Yes, there are books that talk about outstanding practice, there are books that talk about being the leader in the setting, but throughout my research, there has never been an instruction guide… a how to book, a manual on how to prepare for your inspection.

This book will hand-hold you through the journey of the entire process making sure that you are going to shine, you are going to be confident, and you are going to show impact.

Through market research, I have always asked this: what is it that you truly want? I've listened, and I've taken this away and put together this golden nugget to be prepared for your inspection.

There will be some useful tips; some good practice guides, and some outstanding free downloads to help you along the journey.

Throughout the many inspections I have done with Tribal, Ofsted or as part of Jigsaw Early Years Consultancy Quality Improvement Inspection, I have always seen how nervous staff are when walking through the door. I too have been on the end of that.

Through managing many nurseries and group managing six at a time, I used to dread the knock at the door…the showing of the badge and words Ofsted being propelled into me. These were the days of unannounced visits.

The journey through opening your setting, preparing for your inspection and actually enjoying the inspection itself is no mean feat- trust me on this. My thoughts are impelling me to write everything down I know to share.

The motto *sharing is caring* is not only highlighted, but also exemplified in this case. You need to shine for others. This book will help you get fully prepared for that day by being consistently outstanding, every single day.

You can make this happen. Let me help you make it happen.

Enjoy the journey and equally importantly, enjoy the process.

Remember, not everyone will understand your journey

THAT'S FINE.

It's not their journey.

It's yours!

2. THE JUDGEMENTS

The Common Inspection Framework: education, skills and early years was introduced in September 2015. The Common Inspection Framework sets out how Ofsted inspects maintained schools and academies, non-association independent schools, further education and skills provision as well as registered early years settings in England.

The Common Inspection Framework is intended to bring together the inspection of different forms of education and skills. This is from early years all the way through to further education and skills, ensuring consistency throughout the inspection process when children transition from one setting to another.

It might be important to note that we are only focusing on early years within this book. However, the headings are all the identical, so the process will be similar.

If you were inspected between July 2013 and July 2016, you are now back 'in the pot' and need to be prepared for the call. It is evident that it has become harder to achieve *outstanding*, even more so to maintain that grading, with the goal posts being moved with the new inspection framework.

However, if we consistently achieve this on a day to day basis, it will be easier to achieve the grading you desire on the day.

Firstly, let us confirm that we know each child is unique. This is very true to your own setting and also to your own inspection. Your inspector will use the inspection handbook to judge your setting throughout the day and evaluate your practice.

Use this to showcase your own ethos and tone without any inhibition. You will be able to maintain your passion to ensure that children are achieving highly. So when I see on social media comments like 'I've had the call, THEY are coming tomorrow, what do I need to do', it scares me that people write different things ranging from 'My inspector looked at this' to 'Mine didn't, they only wanted to see this'.

Believe you me - your inspector will follow only the guidance which is in the inspection handbook and I cannot emphasise this enough. Your inspector will ask if you have read the handbook and where you would grade yourself using the grade descriptors. Against this backdrop, this book will help bring about clarity of the handbook.

Within the Common Inspection Framework, all areas are covered using the following headings

- Overall effectiveness

- Effectiveness of leadership and management

- Quality of teaching, learning and assessment

- Personal development, behaviour and welfare

- Outcomes for Children

There are 4 judgements:

GRADE 1   ~ OUTSTANDING
GRADE 2   ~ GOOD
GRADE 3   ~ REQUIRES IMPROVEMENT
GRADE 4   ~ INADEQUATE

Your inspector will make use of their professional judgements using the inspection handbook to clarify and use the grade descriptors to give you a grade at the end of your inspection.
They will also look at your setting and see what it would be like for a child in your care, and its potential impact on the children's learning and development.

Good or Outstanding
If you are judged good or outstanding, your next inspection will be within the next cycle, unless you have a serious complaint, which needs to be

investigated and could trigger an unannounced inspection at any time. Good to Outstanding settings next inspections. could take anywhere between 3 and 4 years.

Requires Improvement
If you receive Requires Improvement, you will be re-inspected between 6 and 12 months. This will be announced unless of course you have had a serious complaint which needs to be investigated.

Inadequate
You'll be inspected again within the next 6 months

You will be told what you must do to remain registered, and the date by which it must be done. In addition, your local authority will be informed, which may affect your eligibility for funding; hence it is critically important to get your inspection right.

If you're judged as 'inadequate with enforcement'
You'll be monitored by an inspector. They will visit you to check how you're progressing against the areas you were told needed improvement.

Ofsted may take further action if there's no improvement.

If you have two inspections in a row where you're judged as *inadequate*, Ofsted can actually cancel your registration.

So imagine how hard it is to get *outstanding*. This is the pinnacle of an early years' setting.

According to OFSTED publication dated November 2017, 76% of childcare on non-domestic premises was judged as *good* whereas only 19% were judged as *outstanding*.

As for childminders, 78% of this was judged as *good*, with 14% being declared as *outstanding*. With those figures in mind, it shows how hard it is to achieve the *outstanding* grade.

So, what is it that makes you an *outstanding* setting?

In all fairness, this question is debatable. However, the inspection handbook enables you to use this as an audit tool in order to evaluate your own setting. This is highly recommended.

It is so hard to explain what *outstanding* whilst respecting brevity. So let us start with the facts. Let me just reinforce this: we are all aware that no two children are the same.

They are unique. Similarly, no two settings are the same. So comparing yourself to others is not the way forward.

So, how do we ascertain what *outstanding* is and more importantly, how do we ensure our setting reflects this not only on the inspection day, but in every day practice?

I could go on forever, describing what I think it is…but it may well be different from what you perceive it to be.

I asked this question on social media and not surprisingly, the responses were so diverse.

Here are a few examples:

'Children who are loved and nurtured by every practitioner - practitioners who KNOW their idiosyncrasies and bring out the 'best' in them…'

Mine Conkbayir, author and consultant on Applying Neuroscience to Early Intervention

'That all the hard work and planning I put into running a safe, warm, and nurturing learning environment for the little ones to flourish and fulfil their individual potential has been recognised.'

Jenny Kruk-Strzelecki, Childminder

'Engaged children, staff who have the same vision and expectations, reflective practitioners with evidence of reflections, safeguarding as priority with very knowledgeable staff in this area, supportive community for everyone not just children but staff, management etc. There probably are lots more, but that is some of what I feel it is.'

Carey West, Merton Preschool.

As evident from these responses, we all perceive it to be something different. It indeed is.

It is substantially different to every practice. So, how can we show this on the day of the inspection? My thoughts are that you can only really show what it is, if you are practicing it consistently every day. This is a FACT.

You cannot just turn up, become *outstanding* one fine day and demonstrate your ability to do that consistently to the inspector. They will want to see credible evidence of how you've achieved this. Equally importantly, they will be interested to ascertain how you intend to maintain this for the foreseeable future.

No matter how much you think you do not want *outstanding* and a *good* would suffice, we all know in our hearts that we're ever so anxious to hear those three magical words during the inspection day.

'You are outstanding.'

It is often heard from practitioners that they do not want to get *outstanding*. This is because it is so hard to maintain this grading. At the risk of sounding repetitive, I will say this again: we did *outstanding* practice every day – to the extent that it became easier to maintain this high standard we set for ourselves. Another FACT that must be remembered.

There are many words when writing an inspection report to describe examples of *outstanding* practice…words such as exceptional leadership, inspiring activities which ignite curiosity, highly reflective - to name a few.

But how do we show this in our everyday practice?

To achieve outstanding, you have to ensure you illustrate and include everything that will help you become outstanding in your everyday practice. There is no point just doing it on one day and not the next one. This is not how it works.

Children soon realise that you are doing things differently when the inspector arrives.
I can give you an example of this. I remember one inspection where a practitioner was taking items out of a carrier bag which she had just bought for the day to ensure her Easter activities were the most amazing activities ever.

This was not the case.

The children soon realised that they had things to do which they had not done before. They actually did not know what to do. They waited eagerly for instructions to be handed over by the practitioner. They were handed out pre-cut out templates and were asked to stick items around the edges. There was no discussion about the purpose of the activity. There was no questioning to ignite their learning from the practitioner either.

The children did not know how to use the glue stick; they were looking at it in a perplexed manner as though they had not seen one before. They were given one pair of scissors to share between 3 children; however, as the objects were new, they soon began arguing. The practitioner did not interject or explain to the children there was a need to share. This soon inflamed into a heated conversation with children beginning to shed tears. Behaviour was not managed effectively and children did not know of any boundaries.

That is not something you want to show on the day of inspection.

Needless to say, the *outstanding* grade was moving further away.

So, my advice is to start thinking about your end game right away and you will be able to shine on the day.

So, how are you going to get this grade?

This is where this book comes into its own.

To define *outstanding* would take up a whole book, which is not the intention of the author.

The chapter aims to underpin the fact that *outstanding* means something different to everyone depending on their own perceptions and feelings at a given point in time.

Other examples when are; 'What is outstanding?'

One which stood out in my eyes?

'When I'm standing outside with the warm sun beating on my face and knowing that I have made a positive impact on a little one's life, as well as possibly helping a parent understand their parenting duties and overcoming their OCDs.
Going to infinity and beyond to help a family and their child/children to develop into fine little people that are ready to conquer the world.'

Maimuna Khan,
Childminder

To achieve an *outstanding* grade, you need to have highly effective staff that are singing from your own hymn sheet. Every practitioner needs to be providing the tools and ensuring they are all meeting the unique, innate needs of the child. Your staff need to be passionate and committed to their roles within the team and have a sound understanding of children's developmental needs. This is so important and often missed.

Many years ago, when I struggled to achieve my NNEB, our setting 'bible' was Mary Sheridan. This gave us the framework of all child development from birth to 5 years of age. We knew it backwards, left right and centre.

With my background and experience as a lecturer, I have seen students attend because they have to. Not because they want to. This often makes me wonder: where has the passion for students to *want to* learn more about children's development gone?
Why is this reduced to just another tick box exercise?

During my time as an inspector and a consultant, it became increasingly clear that we are using online assessments to inform us of where children currently are in their developmental stage, and not taking much notice of whether this is right. So my first recommendation would be to ensure that all practitioners in your setting know child development.

Your inspector will want to see that you are knowledgeable in this area. It is the responsibility of the leader or manager to make sure that all standards are not only met, but also kept high; this should be tangible and visible throughout the day. They need to make sure all their team are on board and able to contribute confidently during the day of the inspection.

At the same time, practitioners need to be passionate and committed to their roles and have a firm understanding of children's needs. I repeat this point so that you can reflect on this and take a look at the staff within your setting or yourself as a childminder before deciphering what they know about the stage of development a particular child is in - and how they are going to achieve their next steps.

It is all about the STAFF

Your staffs are the pinnacle to achieving *outstanding;*
let there be no doubt about it. They are the significant
others, who are shepherding children in their journey
of learning and development and the onus is on you
as the manager to ensure that this happening.

But how can you guarantee they are?

As well as having outstanding staff, you will need to
show that you are secure in your EYFS requirements,
in that you should be able to demonstrate your
willingness to work above and beyond what you are
expected to do.

You will need to show that children are making
consistent and significant progress in all areas. If not,
why not and how are you ensuring this is being
monitored?

It is the managers/providers responsibility to ensure
that all the welfare requirements are being adequately
met. To that end, use the Statutory Framework for
the Early Years Foundation Stage (2017) as an audit
tool in order to look at what you are doing under each
heading, and how this impacts on children within
your setting.

If you are a preschool, you may be the manager in
place, but you may also be run by a committee.

Let me just clarify this: if you are a committee run preschool, your committee has a major responsibility on its shoulders.

I have been to so many inspections where the preschool are working really hard to demonstrate the impact and ensure that children's needs are being met, but this comes to a standstill when the committee has not been compliant in their roles.

This can include not informing OFSTED about new committee members to ensuring their DBS are up to date, or not following the correct procedures for the managers' induction. I cannot emphasise this point enough: the committee members have got to be fully involved within their setting. They are classed as providers and therefore, need to take on complete responsibility of the setting. So if you are a committee-run setting, take a step back and ask yourself this question.

Is the committee fully aware of their duties within their roles?

If the answer is no, now is the chance to make those changes and arrange a meeting in order to discuss how important this is to the setting and children.

What is the point?

Are you reading this and already thinking, 'wow, there is too much to know, digest and amend in your setting?'

Do you ever get those days where you think what the whole point is?
When was the last time you took a step back and thought – WOW, today was amazing?

Getting my point? Food for thought, for sure!

Throughout my inspection and consultancy time, I have been so thrilled to see many settings accomplish their *outstanding* rating.

This was their ultimate goal.

Poignantly, the next part of achieving outstanding is to maintain it. So surely, wouldn't it be easier if this was an everyday process and it would be easier to maintain this mind-set and mechanism?

So what do you need to become *outstanding?*

It all starts with a VISION…

Does your setting have a vision?
This vision not only has to be led by an excellent leader; it also needs to be carried forward by a team that is on board – all the way.
I was once taught by an inspiring leader of a group of nurseries,' Speed of the leader, Speed of the team'.

I cannot stress upon this enough.

We all have an idea of where we want to go and the ultimate goal is to achieve that cherished judgement of *outstanding*.

> **"Your vision will become clear only when you can look into your own heart. Who looks outside, dreams; who looks inside, awakes"**
> **Carl Jung**

Starting with your vision,

- Have you ever asked your staff what it is?
- Do your staff team know and live your ethos?
- Why not take this time to ask the question?

If your staff are not misaligned with your mission and vision, then this is potentially the first point of call. Start off with a staff meeting and ask them what they think it is? It is interesting to hear what their views are, and how good it would be if they came up with an idea that can help with promoting that vision.

A staff meeting could be a way of showing staff that you are prepared to listen, which is so important. I have been to settings where practitioners have said they are not listened to. Showing your team you have the ability to respect and assimilate their views can have the same effect as when we listen to children.

It gives them a feeling of self-worth, a sense of value and the much-needed confidence of sharing ideas.

Once you are on board with your setting's vision, this is where the goals are set.

What is your purpose for your setting?

What are you trying to achieve and how are you going to get there? This is a great start for reflecting and evaluating your setting which we will talk about in the next chapter.

Communication

"The art of communication is the language of leadership."
James Humes

The art of effective communication - is this an art?

One of the most important themes of any setting is how a leader or manager communicates to their team.

Now is the time to reflect. List the various ways in which you communicate with your team.

Once you have documented this, look at each method and think about the way this information is received. Put yourselves in their shoes.

How often do you have staff meetings? Do all staff members attend? Do you invite ALL staff members? If not, why not? Can you imagine what it would be like to not be invited to a meeting? Surely, this does not help with the entire staff feeling valued or involved.

What about those who do not attend? How can you ensure they all know what the meeting is about and that they have understood the messages being discussed and relayed?

An example of this happened when I was inspecting a setting and asked a member of staff what they understood about Prevent duty and FGM. The staff member looked at me and said that she was not at the staff meeting when this was being discussed. She then went on to clarify that she does not go to staff meetings as she is 'only cover staff'

Just by thinking about this conversation and watching her face, I could tell she felt undervalued and that she was just there to make sure ratios were being adhered to.

Is that a great start?

Surely making sure that the entire staff involved in day to day running of the setting is paramount to outstanding practice.

Think about this. Would we as practitioners not include all children?

I am hoping you are saying no Vanessa, never. Then why do we feel that we do not need to include the entire staff when it comes to communication?

Now, I totally understand that not everybody can attend meetings due to other commitments, but then it's important to have that discussion with them to help them feel involved in being part of the team.

So the next time you have a meeting, think about everybody in your staff and how you can best communicate with them. Think about the minutes of those meetings; can they be shared with staff via messenger or WhatsApp if needed? Make them feel an inextricable part of the team.

If you are a childminder and have an assistant, this is also the key for your type of setting. How do you ensure they are all working alongside you towards your vision?

You need to show that your staff's views are being listened to and taken on board wherever applicable. This demonstrates a leader as being highly effective - a trait which an *outstanding* judgement stands by.

As part of an effective communication system, we need to have the ability to listen to others before we get our points of view across. We also must take peoples' points of view, successes as well as their apprehensions on board.

"The most basic of all human needs is the need to understand and be understood. The best way to understand people is to listen to them."
Ralph Nichols

Having active listening skills within your setting is important to show you are prepared for any change and remain open to new ideas. This in turn shows that you are working towards an outstanding setting. You must be able to demonstrate a coherent vision, determination and passion for continuous improvement. You also need to be able to consistently reflect and assimilate others' viewpoints, no matter how conflicting they are, to help improve outcomes for children.

After thinking about the way you communicate with staff, think about how you're going to communicate with parents.

- How do you ensure that all parents are being communicated to effectively and consistently?
- Do you involve all parents?

We will talk about this about this further in the chapter on Leadership and Management, but it does give you some food for thought. This is one of the key reporting requirements and is needed to ensure achieving the best outcomes for children.

As a leader, you must show your level of expertise from the very start. You must inspire hope and focus on the children's needs at all times. Their needs are at the forefront of your setting, something that has to be portrayed throughout your entire team. You need to understand and be honest about your journey and know how to take your team through it. At the same time, you need to be extremely reflective and highly engaging in getting things done to achieve the best possible outcomes for children.

Children in your setting need to continually achieve in their chosen areas of learning. If they are not, you need to assess why not, and demonstrate that you are doing everything possible to address the problematic areas.

Notably, *outstanding* does not necessarily mean all children are achieving highly; it's more to do with how you are making sure that they are learning and developing successfully at all times.

Remember, every child is unique and has individual needs which you need to identify and support.

Now it is time for you to reflect upon what you do in your own setting. Go to a quiet, secluded place for about 30 minutes and take an honest look at your setting. I can hear you say in your head, as if I have 30 spare minutes to do this.

If you want to improve your setting then this is a much needed time of reflection.

Use these questions to guide you.
Tick the relevant box after you have answered each question.

Do you and your staff continually listen to the children and take on board their viewpoints, thus enabling them to progress in the areas of learning and development through their own interests?

Consistently	Occasionally	Rarely

Do you and your staff continually enable children in order to choose their own activities to inspire and ignite their curiosity?

Consistently	Occasionally	Rarely

Do your staff members encourage learning in children through scaffolding of language and questioning?

Consistently	Occasionally	Rarely

Are children able to make a choice, able to have a voice and able to choose what they want to do throughout the day?

Consistently	Occasionally	Rarely

Do you and your staff enable children to be independent in their personal development skills through a variety of choices and unrestrained freedom?

Consistently	Occasionally	Rarely

Do you ensure that all staff members use relevant and up to date training to develop children's skills and demonstrate its impact on them in your setting?

Consistently	Occasionally	Rarely

Do you ensure that all children are consistently kept safe through effective risk assessments by ensuring all safeguarding policies are up to date, and ALL staff members are aware of the importance of protecting against different types of abuse, radicalisation and extremism?

Consistently	Occasionally	Rarely

Are all staff members aware of any invisible children in the setting and interact with those children?

Consistently	Occasionally	Rarely

At any point in time, do you find children wandering around the setting looking for things to do?

Consistently	Occasionally	Rarely

Are British Values consistently being promoted in the setting among children by instilling awareness of different cultures and values of every child they are working alongside?

Consistently	Occasionally	Rarely

Is partnership with parents continually being supported and do parents have an understanding of where their children are in their areas of learning and development?

Consistently	Occasionally	Rarely

Do all parents contribute significantly to their children's learning journey? Do you constantly ensure that all parents (depending on their needs) are working in partnership with you?

Consistently	Occasionally	Rarely

Are all staff members aware that the activities they undertake for the children need to have an impact? If so, what is the impact that they hoping to achieve through the children's learning? Are they able to evidence this consistently?

Consistently	Occasionally	Rarely

Are you able to demonstrate that the setting has an ambitious vision?

Consistently	Occasionally	Rarely

Do all staff members have high expectations about what each child can achieve? Do they ensure the compliance of high standards of care and the delivery of provision for children at all times?

Consistently	Occasionally	Rarely

Do you ensure that you staff are ready to improve upon their practice so that they are able to deliver on teaching and learning?

Consistently	Occasionally	Rarely

Do you evaluate the quality of your setting and ensure this is improved through periodic self-evaluation?

Consistently	Occasionally	Rarely

Are the views of parents, children and staff taken into account to make improvements of the setting?

Consistently	Occasionally	Rarely

Do you lead the setting to sustainable success through effective planning, and manage the curriculum learning programme to make sure that all the children have a good start?

Consistently	Occasionally	Rarely

Are children being prepared for school during the next stage of learning?

Consistently	Occasionally	Rarely

Do you actively promote equality and diversity and are trained to tackle negativity?

Consistently	Occasionally	Rarely

Do you make sure that appropriate arrangements are in place to ensure that all children are kept safe from harm, including preventing against radicalisation and extremism?

Consistently	Occasionally	Rarely

Do you make sure that the training is highly effective and improving rapidly through ongoing professional development?

Consistently	Occasionally	Rarely

Do you effectively monitor and identify areas where children may be slow to develop the key skills that they are learning? Furthermore, do you make sure that the gaps in the teaching between different groups of children are negligible or completely eliminated by the time they've gone to school?

Consistently	Occasionally	Rarely

Do you ensure there is a highly effective partnership that not only involves with your parents, but also with outside agencies to ensure that the improvement of provision and outcomes for children is maximised at all times?

Consistently	Occasionally	Rarely

So with using these questions, they should give you a good basis to look at your practice and make improvements.

The Unique word again!

To reiterate, your practice is unique to you and you only. Not all approaches, accreditations or theories are suitable for every setting.

Although having an Ofsted inspection and guidance is highly important for us, they are not able to judge us on the way we deliver practice in our setting unless it breaches welfare requirements and as long as we are able to demonstrate the impact our teaching is having on our children's learning

We need to show that we are providing a welcoming, nurturing and evolving practice which meets the needs and outcomes of all children walking through our door. We need to grow as a setting and discover what works well for us and our children. You all know your children better than anyone else does.

Remember that.

We have a range of techniques that are best suited to our learning styles of children, and we need to ensure that this quality is of the highest form.

By meeting the needs of all welfare requirements and the Statutory Framework for the EYFS, you are well on your way of showcasing your setting. Once this has been achieved, you need to look at your practice step by step so as to make sure that this is effective for all children, and not just the ones who are exceeding.

What about the ones who need a little help, the invisible child who does not give you a stressful day, or the one who wanders around the room looking for things to do? The one who rarely engages in conversation with you unless you are asking them a question.

Find those children and encourage them to connect with you and your setting. This ensures you are aware that all children are unique and treat them accordingly.

Getting it right first time was published in July 2013 to help with achieving and maintaining high quality provision of early years. Even though it is over 5 years old, it is still used today by inspectors. We should be actively promoting this document in our settings to give us some understanding of how to get it right the first time.

Areas are outlined to ensure that settings are aware of what is needed to make a setting *good* or *outstanding*.

Strong leadership is crucial. It drives up the quality of a setting's work and ensures all children are encouraged to reach their full potential.

We will discuss the attributes of strong leaders further on within this book.

3. WHAT IS THE POINT OF SELF-EVALUATION?

A rumour has been doing the rounds that self-evaluation is scrapped with Ofsted. This is **not** true

The only thing which has been scrapped is its uploading to the portal.

In order to banish the way we self-evaluate, would be to change the whole Inspection Handbook, Guidance and Framework. This will not happen.

Every section of the Inspection Handbook says we need to evaluate Leadership and management, teaching learning and assessment, personal development behaviour and welfare and outcomes for children.

Another term for self –evaluation is self-assessment. So what does this mean?

"Self-evaluation will help you to consider the best way to create, maintain and improve your setting, so that it meets the highest standard and offers the best experience for young children."
(Page 4 of Early Years Self-evaluation Form Guidance, OFSTED)

The Early Years Inspection Handbook (2015 Reference no: 150068) states:

'The provider MUST demonstrate how they evaluate their service and strive for continuous improvement'. (p7)

The inspector must look at all relevant documentation and see the self-evaluation document if the provider has not already submitted it. (p11)

'Leaders and managers of settings should have an accurate view of the quality of their provision and know what to improve upon. This view should be summarised in their self-evaluation. Inspectors will use this self-evaluation to evaluate how well a setting knows its strengths and weaknesses, and how it can improve or maintain its high standards' (p15)

When asking the question on social media, the responses were all different albeit with the same meaning:

'Reflection on how you work, ways to improve your setting and how we work.
What specific measures can we undertake to achieve this.'

Anna Matthews, Childminder, Hampshire

'Evaluating your current position. Reflecting on what else you want to achieve and having ideas on how you are going to achieve these.'

Sarah Warne, Childcare and Education Manager, Happy Days Nurseries (South West) Ltd

'Reflecting on practice to improve skills. To try a new approach and implement new strategies so that may work better next time.'

Donna O'Shea, Lead educator, Pelican Waters Early Learning Centre, Queensland, Australia

'Not forgetting what you do well as well as areas for development'

Anna Wright, Owner Paint Pots Pre-school and Nursery (10 settings)

Reflection of own practice and behaviours, identifying strengths and areas for improvement.

Laura Staff, Teaching assistant/trainee Early Years practitioner, The Arches Primary School, Chester

Valuing strengths, recognising opportunities and reformulating for continuous progress!

Sarah Hawkins

Self-evaluation means that we need to look at what we are doing in the present and think about our strengths and weaknesses... how can we improve on this?

Every day, whether you are an Early Years setting or not, you are evaluating what you are doing and how you would do things differently next time. Think about the time when you make dinner using a recipe. What happens when you serve this at the table and you all begin tasting what you have cooked? Do you think it is just fine, or do you often feel what can I do to make it taste better next time?

Everyone needs to be reflective and evaluate their practice. How else are we going to improve on the way we do things?

Would it be a shocker for you to know that at the end of my inspections, I would often ask how I could improve on the way I inspected?

The look on the managers' faces when being asked that question was sometimes that of pure horror. The question was: why would you (as an inspection) want to know that?

Here's the thing. Why wouldn't I want to know?

As a lecturer and trainer, we reflect on every lesson or training; we ask ourselves what went well and how we can make improvements next time. If we don't ask ourselves those hard questions, how can we improve?

Ask yourself this question:

- Can you improve on managing of your setting?
- Can you improve on working in partnership with parents or others?
- Can you improve on the quality of teaching within your setting?
- If yes, how so? Do you ask staff how you can improve?

That is a big question but actually gives real insight into you as a leader or manager. If you are open to change, then this *is* the way forward. If not, I would suggest you look for another career. Early Years is very reflective and we need to be constantly doing this.

So with that being said, how do we do this to show IMPACT?... There is that word again... maybe I should explain the meaning of that word before moving on any further. Impact here means to have a strong effect on someone or something. So, what do you do in your setting that has an enduring effect on a child's learning and development?

Examples could be:

The childminder uses photographs of children and their family members on the display board. Children are eager to name and talk about those photographs.

Based on the sentence above, the impact is that the children are able to feel a sense of belonging and self-worth.

Another example:

Staff make accurate assessments through the teaching opportunities every day. Children are able to choose and talk about the dinosaurs in the sand tray.

The impact of this is the development of children's confidence and speaking skills through their own interests. They are engaging in questioning and using their critical thinking skills to spark curiosity.

Back to self-evaluation - whichever setting you are in, whether it's a day nursery, preschool or as a childminder - we need to do this. So with the news of Ofsted having scrapped the uploading to the portal, we do need to show we do this consistently, every single day. I can hear many of you thinking that this has left a huge gap, but how can we show this? Remember, at the beginning of this book I said that you need to shine...now is your chance.

Think about how you can show what you do and the improvements you make every day to make sure the children are attaining those high outcomes.
Ofsted does now say that you do not need to get this documented but why not kill two birds with one stone and create a document where you can show tangible evidence to parents, visitors, new staff on

interviews - as well as your inspector? Why not create a floor book for each room to demonstrate how they are evaluating their own practice.

Throughout my travels, I have seen many versions of this and that's where the motto of *sharing is caring* comes into play. As an inspector, I would always ask how settings are evaluated. This did not necessarily mean it needed to be written; however, if it was, it did suggest they were making it a point to record and show whatever they needed to do next. This certainly made a positive difference to the inspection process.

When asked the question: 'Do you struggle to self–evaluate and if so, why?' - The answers were very clear.

No, I always look at something and think of a different approach or system. But I do struggle with writing it down!
Donna O'Shea, Lead educator, Pelican Waters Early Learning Centre, Queensland, Australia

Time.
Anna Wright, Owner of Paintpots Nurseries, Southampton

I think I am constantly evaluating but the recording I struggle with. I have started jotting scribbled notes in my diary bullet journal style and that works for me. It may make no sense to anyone but me but it beats banging my head filling in a template that bears no resemblance to my normal way of doing things just to please the powers that be.

When Ofsted come they may or may not like my style but I can talk the hind legs off a donkey about why I do what I do and the impact changes have made so, hopefully that will be enough. I am one little me so I can do no more and I'm good with that.

Lynda Hall, Childminder, Basingstoke

If these are your issues, let's see if we can make this process easier for you.

This is your setting and your time to shine. During your inspection, you will be slightly stressed and be very aware of your staff, children, parents and even the inspector on the day. So let us use the Self-evaluation to say the following

What?

So What?

Now What?

Thank you Driscoll (1994): for providing us with this simple tool of how to reflect and evaluate.

This means looking at what you do, what was the impact and thinking about what you are going to do to change it in order to improve.

My suggestion would be to break the sections into areas where you are being inspected, as this will go a long way in ensuring that you are covering each section.

For example:

REFLECTION DOCUMENT		
Leadership and Management		
1	Supervisions and Appraisal	Date
	Use this section to demonstrate how often you deliver supervisions, and give examples of what actions you have asked your staff to achieve.	
	Also specify what IMPACT this has had on the setting. For example using the DRISCOLL method	
	WHAT During one staff member's supervisions, we discussed how assessments were not being recorded accurately and observations were not of high quality	
	SO WHAT This was having an impact of not being able to share accurate information with parents and to inform future practice in activities for the children	
	NOW WHAT We decided to put this staff member on an observation, assessment and planning course in the Spring to hone the ability to track effectively. The staff member	

	attended the course and delivered a training session to the other team members at the staff meeting. This was to help them have confidence in what they had learnt and share this with the entire staff. Within three weeks, staff members were tracking more effectively and children's next steps were accurately being documented. At the same time, children's learning was also being extended	
2	**Now think of other ways using the method of DRISCOLL**	
	Quality of your provision **WHAT** **SO WHAT**	

	NOW WHAT	
3	How children are kept safe in your provision? **WHAT** **SO WHAT**	

	NOW WHAT	
4	How do you work in partnership with parents and other agencies? **WHAT** **SO WHAT**	

	NOW WHAT	
5	How do you use coaching/mentoring of trainees and students or your assistants **WHAT** **SO WHAT**	

	NOW WHAT	
6	How do you use any additional funding, including the early years pupil premium? How does this impact the children's learning? **WHAT** **SO WHAT**	

	NOW WHAT	

This is one example of good practice:

If you ever felt you wanted to accentuate the strengths of your setting even more, why not develop a scrapbook idea, which makes it possible for each section to be evaluated on a weekly basis?

Divide the scrapbook into the following sections:

- Leadership and Management
- Teaching learning and Assessment
- Personal development, behaviour and welfare
- Outcomes for children

Every day, you are taking pictures of the children learning and developing, so why not use this format to demonstrate how you can evaluate? This pictorial journey depicts what you are doing now and its impact. Why not go one stage further and say how you can improve this next time? Using the Curiosity Case as an example:

Courtesy of Roseville Nursery, Leeds

What
Children were interested in what they needed to take on holiday.
So What
They were able to engage in conversations with their peers and take turns in listening to each other, recalling past events.

They talked about how they were going on a holiday and solved a problem using the case to be able to fit in and row to their chosen country.

Now What

Investigation on sinking and floating and what materials are needed to do this. Using questioning such as what would happen if?
How can we make it float?
How can we stop it from sinking?

This shows an example of how you can evaluate with impact. If you are a day nursery, consider giving your settings rooms their own learning journal to showcase what they do well and the things they can do to ensure children are continually developing.

This would not only help with your whole evaluation process in your setting; it would also give the team a chance to be involved and take autonomy of their room. In turn, this would make sure that all your staff members are on board with the whole process as opposed to leaving this to you as the owner or manager.

4. THE CALL

The best preparation for good work tomorrow is to do good work today

Elbert Hubbard

How do you feel when you get the call?

- Anxious
- Scared
- Nervous
- Irritable
- Excited

Why do you think that is how you feel? Is it because this is your first inspection, or because you have had a bad experience? Regardless, you need to showcase your setting throughout the process. This is your one and only chance to show what your setting and staff are made of to the Ofsted inspector.

When will you get that chance again?

Remember, the inspector is a human being too who has a family at home just like you and me - and is only doing his/her job! They want children to achieve best outcomes and can only judge you based on the time they are with you.

With that in mind….SMILE…it will and does make the day go better.

So think about when answering the settings phone during the day. Is it usually chaotic and the noise is carried through to where you are answering the phone?

Do you ever think 'I will leave the phone to ring and I am sure they will ring back?' Yes, people usually do. But one word of caution: the inspector will only make three phone calls to try and make contact with you. If you do not answer the phone on each of these three occasions, they are well within their rights to arrive unannounced!

The inspector will usually call the day before around lunch time…yes,
I know that is your busiest time. We have devised this chapter to make you well prepared and confident when the call is made.

Remember, preparation is the key!

If you are a childminder, the call will come approximately five days before your inspection. You will be asked which days you have children's in the Early Years age range.

First impressions definitely count, so make sure that whoever answers the telephone knows how to respond to 'That Call.' Do you have a standard way of answering the telephone? Think about how first impressions are made when you do.

The inspector will explain that they are visiting you the next day (or within the next five days if you are a childminder) and inform you about the time they will be arriving. Make sure to ask their name. This is so important as it will set you at ease and this will also set the tone of the inspection.

At this point you will be asked questions and it would be good to have the information readily available. Some of the questions will include:

- ✓ How many children currently do you have on Roll?
- ✓ How many children do you have in on the day of inspection?
- ✓ How many staff do you have working on that day?
- ✓ How many children do you have with EAL?
- ✓ How many children do you have with additional needs?
- ✓ How many 2 year old funded children do you have?

✓ Do you have any children with EYPP?

We have provided you with a prompt sheet which will ensure that you are very prepared to answer these questions.

Points to remember when they call:

- Remain calm
- Remain polite and professional
- Stay positive and your confidence will shine through
- Ask for their name and record this
- Ask for their car details as this will help with any car parking issues in case there is a space constraint in your setting
- Ask them if they require lunch. Usually, an inspector will take some time off to eat their lunch if the inspection is a day-long process. This gives them and you some time for a breather. They are human after all!
- Ensure your documentation is ready for the day of inspection

Here is a list of the documentation you will need to have ready on the day of inspection. Being prepared for this will make it easier for you to stand out whilst also enabling the inspector to spend more time with the children and staff and make observations. This will help you to excel.

- Current staff list and their qualifications, including paediatric first aid certificates
- Documentation showing routine staffing arrangements, such as a rota or staffing structure on a daily basis
- A list of the children who will be present at the setting during the time of inspection (if not shown on the register)
- The Disclosure and Barring Service (DBS) records and any other documentation summarising the checks, vetting and employment arrangements of the entire staff working at the setting. This should include the committee if you work in a pre-school
- All logs recording accidents, exclusions, children taken off roll and incidents of poor behaviour
- All logs recording incidents of discrimination, including any racist incidents
- A complaint log and/or evidence of any complaints and resolutions. This should be inclusive of any complaint
- Safeguarding and child protection policies/certificates
- Risk assessment, fire safety and other health & safety related policies
- A list of any referrals made to the designated person for safeguarding in addition to brief details of the resolutions

- A list of children who are an open case to social care/children's services and for whom a multi-agency plan is put in place
- Information about the supervision of staff/assistants; this should include childminding assistants
- Information about training and/or career professional development of staff
- Any reports of external evaluation of the setting
- A register or list showing the date of birth of all children on roll.

(See download PDF for the free tick list)

Make sure the whole setting is aware that you are expecting an inspector, including staff members who are absent on the day of the call but are supposed to be working on the day of the inspection. Remember the motto of 'speed of the leader speed of the team.' All team members need to feel valued and made to feel that they are as much a part of this journey as you are.

Gone are the days now when inspectors just arrive on your doorstep. (Unless it's a compliance visit) There is much debate over whether this is right or wrong. I have been on the receiving end of both and can safely say that the stress of knowing inspectors are coming is far greater than the stress of opening the door to them.

The whole purpose of the call is to clarify the registration of your setting and any changes made to the registration. These are duly noted and you will need to produce evidence that you have notified Ofsted about the changes when the inspector arrives.

As an inspector, the most common faux pas I have experienced is with committee run pre-schools. The amount of times I have arrived at a setting, having pre-checked the Portal for the names of nominated persons and committee members, only to find changes on the day that matters.

The chair of committees needs to realise the importance of informing Ofsted of ALL changes. This includes the EY2 form.

Failure to do so will definitely have an impact on the grade of your inspection even before the inspector goes any further to see what a great job you do.

An example of such report would read like this:

'The provider failed to ensure that the relevant information about new committee members was sent to Ofsted to enable them to complete suitability checks.'

The provider in this case, as it is a Committee run pre-school, is the Committee. I cannot stress how important it is for the Committee to understand they need to have secure knowledge of the setting they are a member of.

This could lead to a Grade 3 (*Requires improvement*) or Grade 4 (*Inadequate*) rating if this has an impact on the safeguarding requirements.

Before the inspection -the inspector will check the following:

- They will see which register your setting is on and confirm the same with you. In case of any ambiguity, the inspector will check this with the applications team at the help desk.
- They will confirm all pieces of information regarding individuals connected to the registration
- Any lines of enquiry which will be shown on their portal; this includes the recommendations based on previous inspection, any safeguarding concerns, and any complaints that may have been recorded. These would be also be shown on the Portal and the event details which the inspector downloads before visiting you. Only Ofsted has access to this information.
- Any previous reports
- Any published information such as any monitoring letters sent out to you. They will check your website if you have one
- If you have a social media page this will be checked. Please be very mindful of the information you include on your page. If you are showing the faces of children, the

inspector will want to confirm that you have secured written parental permission.

Please do remember that your personal page does have a linkage to your business page. Whatever is put on your social media page will be shared worldwide. Think about how this may look to the general public.

You will also need to speak to the parents and inform them that you are going to be inspected.

Parents need to be given the chance to speak to the Ofsted Inspector. As one of the reporting requirements, this is indicative of a good working partnership. Your inspector needs to be able to write how well you work with parents and others. If your parents are unable to talk to the Ofsted Inspector, why not ask them to write you a testimonial?

It all builds to the body evidence and forms part of you evaluating your practice (see Chapter 2).

Tips for the day of inspection:

- ✓ Do not panic
- ✓ Be prepared
- ✓ Breathe
- ✓ Remember that you know your children well; you just need to explain the same to the Ofsted Inspector. They do not know the children at all, so will want to know what you know

✓ Think about if the Ofsted Inspector was asked to be the key person to your children instead of you on a particular day; would they know which stage the child is at based on your observations, assessment and planning?

This is a really important aspect to be aware of… all children need to be observed, assessed and planned for at all times. There should be no gaps in their learning.

5. LEADERSHIP AND MANAGEMENT

Leadership and management assume great importance in Early Years settings. To be a good leader, you need to get your team on your side and take the journey with you.

'We must be the change we wish to see in the world'
Mahatma Gandhi

Without your team being a part of your ethos, you will struggle to achieve as much as you want to. The inspector will want to see how the effectiveness of your leadership and management impacts your setting. This chapter will break down the areas that must be demonstrated/described and give examples of what you can showcase.

There are a number of questions you need to ask yourself, so that you are confident in your answers.

These answers will facilitate the judgement of leadership and management by evaluating the level of the following:

- How do you demonstrate the vision of your setting? Do you have high expectations of what the children in your setting can achieve and ensure that you have high standards of care for children?

- How do you improve your staff's practice of teaching & learning and provide effective levels of supervisions so as to ensure that you are promoting appropriate professionalism?

- How do you evaluate the quality of your setting and ensure that the accounts of the staff, children and parents are taken into consideration to make sure you are improving?

- How do you provide learning programmes and a curriculum that meets the relevant Statutory Requirements during the Early Years Foundation Stage whilst also taking into account and addressing issues relating to the children's interests?

- How do you successfully plan and manage the curriculum/learning programmes so that children get a good start in their learning journey and are well prepared for the next stage of their learning as well as bigger picture before being ready for school?

- How do you constantly promote equality and diversity ensuring that British Values are demonstrated and that poor behaviour towards others is acted upon? This needs to include bullying and discrimination. The required learning outcomes of different groups of children also need to be demonstrated and met.

- How do you make sure that you meet all the statutory and other government requirements regarding the protection of children, promoting their welfare and are able to prevent radicalisation and extremism?

Considering the following guidelines, we will break down each section, specify what this means and how you can ensure that you are meeting the needs of the requirements with impact.

Safeguarding

One of the reporting criteria which an inspector will take a close look at would be: 'How effective is your safeguarding within your setting?' Their aim is to ensure that you are providing a safe and secure environment for the children to thrive in. They will consider how well leaders and managers have created a culture of vigilance where children's welfare is accorded top priority. In addition, they will also evaluate if there are any concerns that these are acted upon swiftly.

Safeguarding covers a huge range, which not only comes under the view of Leadership and Management area, but also personal, development behaviour and welfare. So, if you have a safeguarding concern at your inspection, do know that this will impact both judgements in these areas.

Settings will need to consider the Working together to Safeguard children (2018) and Information sharing for practitioners (2018) please note the date as the new versions are needed to be used as well as Prevent Duty. These need to be digested and used within your own safeguarding policy.

There are five main aspects the inspectors look for under the safeguarding remit. These are:

- How leaders, managers and providers (this includes a committee) ensure a positive culture and ethos, where becomes an important part of everyday life within a setting. This also includes all levels of training in safeguarding

- The effectiveness of the safeguarding policies, including safer recruitment and vetting processes

- The quality of the safeguarding practice where staff are aware of the types and signs of abuse whilst ensuring that the welfare of all children is kept at the forefront

- The response time if any safeguarding concerns are raised. This is so important and often compliant visits are raised because concerns were not actioned quick enough or to the right organisation.

- The quality of support when working with multi agencies around a plan for a child.

We will cover each section and explain what needs to be evidenced throughout the course of your practice.

Firstly, how does the committee, leader or yourself, if a childminder, ensure a safeguarding culture and ethos is promoted throughout every day practice.

Inspectors will want to see the following:

- Policies that have been reviewed regularly and demonstrate when new legislation/documentation has been released along with its visible impact on the policy

- Staff members are supported to have an awareness of signs that a child may have been neglected or abused and have knowledge of

'What to do if you're worried a child is being abused'

- All staff members, leaders, committee members and volunteers must receive appropriate safeguarding training; this needs to be updated regularly. All need to know their responsibilities regarding how to protect children from harm.

There needs to be a Designated Safeguarding Lead (DSL) in charge of safeguarding with the appropriate level of training, who fully understands that it is their responsibility to ensure all children are kept safe, and that all staff members are up to date with their training and remain confident in the knowledge to recognise any concerns that they may have.

The Statutory Framework for the Early Years Foundation Stage effective from 3rd April 2017 states under Section 3:

3.2. 'Providers must take all necessary steps to keep children safe and well. The requirements in this section explain what early years providers must do to: safeguard children; ensure the suitability of adults who have contact with children; promote good health; manage behaviour; and maintain records, policies and procedures.'

As well as:

3.5. 'A practitioner must be designated to take lead responsibility for safeguarding children in every setting.

Childminders must take the lead responsibility themselves. The lead practitioner is responsible for liaison with local statutory children's services agencies, and with the LSCB. They must provide support, advice and guidance to any other staff on an ongoing basis, and on any specific safeguarding issue as required. The lead practitioner must attend a child protection training course that enables them to identify, understand and respond appropriately to signs of possible abuse and neglect'

If you are a childminder, you are the designated safeguarding lead and hence, must take on the responsibility yourself. You need to ensure that your training is suitable to meet the needs of the safeguarding of children.

The inspector will want to speak to the Designated Safeguarding Lead to ensure that they are confident in the referral process of any safeguarding concerns. When asked questions, they will have to know the process confidently, be thorough in their knowledge of the setting's safeguarding policy and ensure that they have given the inspector the confidence they know the procedure if they had any concerns.

If any referrals have been made, the inspector will want to check whether this was shared with the local authority and written secured records were shared in a timely way. You do have 48 hours to share the information, but as a qualified safeguarding instructor, I can say that it is paramount to get those forms to the correct agency as quickly as possible. Your policy also needs to state the time, within which you need to have all the documentation sent to the correct agencies.

Settings must also be risk assessed and this needs to be demonstrated to your inspector. You have to protect babies and children and to ensure that age appropriate reasonable risks, form an adequate part of their development.

This section also covers positive behaviour as well as being present in Personal development, behaviour and welfare; the inspector will want to see how effective you use de-escalation techniques and strategies to ensure that the needs of individual children are met. All incidents will need to be recorded and effectively monitored; at the same time, the management of behaviour will need to be seen as effective.

With this in mind, you may also want to think of other ways in which children are able to self-regulate their emotions via co regulation strategies that you use. This will ensure children are able to show resilience.

Prevent Duty
The inspector will also focus on the knowledge from staff regarding their understanding on Prevent Duty and FGM.

As an ex-inspector, there were questions I needed to ask and record as pieces of evidence to ensure that staff members were aware of how to recognise any signs and report the same to the Designated Safeguarding Lead.

Examples of potential questions include:

1.   What does the Prevent Duty protect children from?

2. How would a childcare setting demonstrate that they are protecting children from being drawn into terrorism?

3. In what existing policies would you expect to read about the Prevent Duty?

4. If you suspected a child was being radicalised, who would you report your concerns to?

5. What signs would you look out for if you suspected a child was being radicalised?

6. Can you name all of the British Values that should be embedded into your practice?

Vetting process
Staff as well as volunteers need to be carefully selected when joining your setting and should be vetted in accordance to the statutory requirements. This will need to be demonstrated in your application and recruitment procedure. The inspector will also speak to staff in your settings to ensure that the stated procedure is being followed. Usually, conversations are initiated with the newest member of your team.

If you have assistants as a childminder, it is also important for you to show that they applied for the post and highlight the steps taken by you to ensure they are suitable. This needs to be recorded and demonstrated to your inspector.

Partnership working

'TEAM WORK
Coming together is a beginning
Keeping together is progress
'Working together is success'
Henry Ford

Working together in partnership with others is very high on the agenda during your inspection. How do you ensure that all parents feel they are being valued, interacting and engaging in their children's development, and that you are listening to their voice? How do you work with outside agencies to ensure that children's needs are being met?

The Early Years Foundation Stage (2017) states:

The EYFS seeks to provide **partnership working** between practitioners and with parents and/or carers.'

If you can honestly say that you have all parents on board in your setting, and that you are consistently working together to improve outcomes for children, this chapter is not for you.

However I truly feel that we need to ensure we are engaging with all parents and carers and have strategies in place to make this happen.
Examples of the efficacy with which partnership is shown in an Ofsted report might look like this:

"The childminder enthusiastically works with parents and shares ideas for home learning through home link books and activities. This actively encourages an excellent partnership with parents. She is excellent at communicating information with parents regarding their children's care, learning and development.'
Nicola Facey, Childminder

'Partnerships with parents are excellent. Information sharing between staff and parents is highly effective. The parent's involvement in their child's learning ensures that children's needs are quickly identified and successfully met. Highly active links with the local schools and other settings create a tremendous sense of belonging for children and their families.'
Shawford and Compton Preschool, Winchester

Both of these settings showed how their partnership with parents was *outstanding*. They both knew their parents needs and styles, which allowed them to help the foundations of partnership. Parents' involvement was developed through a variety of methods in order to make it highly effective.

Right from the time when a child first starts at your setting, you should inform parents of who their key person is. This is mandatory. The Statutory

Framework of the Early Years Foundation (2017) states:

1.1 *'Providers must inform parents and/or carers of the name of the key person, and explain their role, when a child starts attending a setting.'*

Think about what you do in your setting.
Do you wait for a child to be given a key person?
What makes you decide on the key person?
As per the regulations, it is a 'must'.

Children need to build attachments to their key person who will then ensure they are forming safe and secure relationships with their key child. In turn, this will give them the basis to know this child well enough and be ready to develop their learning through the environment.

2.1. *'Assessment plays an important part in helping parents, carers and practitioners to recognise children's progress, understand their needs, and to plan activities and support.'*

How do you do this? What method do you use to observe, assess and plan for a child? How do you ensure parents are involved in this process?

Do you use an online tracking tool and give parents the log in to see where their child is in their development?

How do you ensure parents understand how this works?

Why not invite parents to an evening's training about how the online tool works and use this time to underpin the importance of working in tandem whilst assessing their children?

I understand that it can be a time issue, with parents being so busy, but there is nothing worse than having this as a recommendation in your report when something *could be done* about it.
Do your parents know that this is a reporting requirement and would affect your judgement grade? If not, let them know.
I am sure if they knew, they would do everything they could to help you gain the rightful judgement during your inspection.

There have been many settings which I have inspected. When managers are asked the question about how they work in partnership with parents, they say they do their best to encourage this, but not all parents want to be involved in these conversations. Firstly, when I used to hear this, I would think that you are giving yourself a recommendation for your own report. So, before you start answering this question, think about all the ways in which you encourage parents to share their children's learning development. Please do not focus on parents who don't. Think positively about all the parents who do.

Another question you may like to ask yourself is - how do you work with other settings? Again, this is a reporting requirement and hence, will be asked. It will also be followed up with clarification from different staff members.

Think about how you do this? Do you send emails? Do you make phone calls? Do you share learning journals via your on-line tracking system? Whatever you do - does this work and is this two-way communication?

Again, another 'faux pas' is to say to the inspector that you have tried to contact the other preschool, childminder, nursery but you did not get any response.

Do you recognise that in your setting? Have you tried all strategies to engage with other settings? Can you honestly say that you have exhausted all options?

If you are not receiving any responses from other settings, why not give them a call and be honest with them. Explain that one of the reporting requirements within the Statutory Framework is to work with other settings and share development, strategies and needs of the child. Explain that as part of this process, you would like to work with them and explore the possibility of sending end of term reports to each other that can be used as a piece of evidence to show the inspector.

I cannot stress enough how important it is for each setting to work together. This is *good* and *outstanding* practice, but also it shows you are according top priority to the child's needs.

So thinking about outside agencies, do you know who you can work with and how to find out if you are able to receive help? This can be a mind-boggling question.

In many leadership and management discussions, the majority of managers and childminders, when asked this question, would say the same thing; 'We have tried to contact agencies but with limited funding they are not able to help us'. What is sad is that we all know children's' needs have to be met but this may not be happening due to the funding crisis.

With the closure of children centres and the cutting off of your local councils funding, you may not be able to access the support you need. For example, for a child with behavioural issues, do you have a portage service which can come out and support you? If the answer is no, have you thought about contacting the local health visitor as they may have a direct line, or may be able to help you by visiting and giving you some new, untried strategies?

If you have concerns about a child's communication skills, are you able to contact the speech and language therapist of your local children's services and ask for some help? Quite often, the answer is 'there's a waiting list.' My advice would be not to delay in sourcing help as soon as you find yourself facing some concerns. I am sure you will have kept records of observations, so when they do hopefully visit, they would be able to see that you have tried everything in your capacity to help that child to secure the required support. Again, please make sure parents are kept in the loop with this linking with other agencies.

There has to be a way of receiving additional help if needed, and you as the settings leader or manager will need to find that way. Children's needs must come first.

Questions to consider when working in partnership

How do you ensure that your parents are happy? – These questions should start to provoke your thinking about what you do with your current set of parents and what is it that you can do to be in sync with the parents' understanding of happiness.

Do you use questionnaires and if yes, how often do you send these out?
What do you do with that information and do you inform parents about the answers to the questions as a summary of your findings?

Doing so would help parents feel they are being listened to so when asked by your inspector whether their views are taken into consideration; the answer would be a confident YES.

What about a comment box? Do you use a form of these and encourage parents to place their comments? How often do you look inside this box! Do remember that there is no point in providing one of these if you are unwilling to take action on anything written on the comments. Also, you may be pleasantly surprised some of these comments may be positive! How great would that be to share with your team, letting them know they feel valued?

Think about this: Do you consider the views of outside agencies? Think about the ways you gather information from outside agencies. Do you have a good rapport with them and how do you ensure congruity between your/their thought process whilst taking them seriously? This again assumes great importance for working with partners.

Do you record these and again what do you do with this information and how do you show the impact that this has made on your setting?

Remember though that when you are sharing information with outside agencies, parents need to sign to say they have agreed to this. This needs to be collected at the very outset when children start with you. Think about if they do not agree to sign the form.

Do they have a valid reason for this? If not and parents do not agree on the information sharing form, this does need to be recorded also.

Is this a cause for concern? And what are you going to do with this information?

Parents and carers need to be aware that if you have concerns about the well-being of their children, this becomes a 'duty of care' and you need to report this immediately regardless of whether they have signed the consent or not.

How well do you work with others to help you understand a child's development and ascertain ways of improving their learning? Think of the way you work with other settings' childminders, preschools or nurseries regarding working together on a child's development. How do you record this and show its impact on the child and your setting?

Do you share children's Progress check at 2 with the Health visitor or do you only give a copy to parents. Think about if parents do not pass a copy of this very important document to the Health visitor.

There may be key points and concerns which may not be communicated effectively. So, my advice would be to share this with the Health visitor as part of your ongoing working in partnership with outside agencies.

Have you considered encouraging parents to complete questionnaires to help you evaluate your practice.
If not, why not?

Example of a questionnaire

Dear parents,
As part of our self-evaluation, we are constantly striving to improve upon our practice and would appreciate your willingness to share your views on this. All answers will be treated anonymously.
Please put a cross in the box as your answer

We will collate the information and send out the report to you summarising our findings and any actions that are needed.

Scale:

Strongly Agree = 4
Agree = 3
Disagree = 2
Strongly disagree = 1

Statement	4	3	2	1
The induction procedure helped my child to settle nicely within the setting				
My child is happy to come to the setting				

My child feels safe at the setting				
My child is making good progress within his/her room				
We are aware of his/her next steps of learning				
We feel we are adequately involved with his/her care and education in the setting				
We know who our child's key person is				
We feel we can talk to the key person regarding our child's learning				
We are kept well informed about our child's learning and receive reports termly				
Our child's behaviour is being managed effectively				

The setting helps our child feel confident				
The learning experiences acquired by our child at the setting are at the appropriate level for them				
Our child is encouraged to be healthy and physically active				
The setting gives us ideas on how to support our child's learning at home				
Our child was duly supported when they started at the setting before moving to a new room				
All staff members are approachable and we feel that we can freely ask any questions we have				

Any further comments	
Date :	

Thank you for taking the time to complete this questionnaire.

This is just an example and the wording may need to amended to suit your settings needs. The Ofsted inspector may want to speak to a parent about the questionnaire and possible ask a couple of questions to see how happy they are with your setting.

Examples of these questions may include:

1. How long has your child been at the setting?
2. How often do they come to the setting?
3. What made you choose this setting for your child?
4. What was the settling in procedure like for you and your child?
5. Do you know where policies are kept and have you received a copy of these?
6. Do you know who your child's key person is?
7. How often do you discuss your child's development?
8. What information is passed on during the pick-up times?

9. Do you know who to approach if you have any concerns?

10. If you have any concerns about the manager or owner, who would you go to?

11. Did you know Ofsted have a complaint number you can call? The inspector will always direct parents to the Ofsted complaint number which needs to be displayed on the parents' notice board.

12. Would you recommend the setting to others and why?

13. It is a good practice to ask parents questions about your setting especially because they are also your partners.

So why not give them a questionnaire to complete as well on a regular basis. This will not only make them feel valued, but will also help iron out any concerns which may arise and allow communication to run effectively. Again, these questionnaires can be answered anonymously.

As well as questionnaires for parents why not give your staff time to answer a version also.

Example of staff questionnaire

Dear staff member,
As part of or self-evaluation, we are constantly striving to improve upon our practice and would appreciate your willingness to share your views on

this. All answers will be treated anonymously. Please place a cross in the box as your answer

We will collate the information and send out the report to you summarising our findings and any actions that are needed.

Scale:

Strongly Agree = 4
Agree = 3
Disagree = 2
Strongly disagree = 1

Statement	4	3	2	1
I find it rewarding to be a member of the team at this setting				
I feel a valued part of the settings community				
I am encouraged to learn and share practice from my colleagues within my setting				
I am given the chance to share best practice with colleagues from other settings				

I have a clear understanding of the vision of the setting				
I am supported to engage in professional learning				
Staff members treat each other with respect				
Staff members treat children with respect				
Children are encouraged to treat each other with respect				
Parents and staff treat each other with respect				
Staff members are aware on how to manage children's behaviour				
Staff members at all levels communicate effectively with each other				
Staff members effectively engage all parents in their child's learning				

The setting is well led and managed				
All children are engaged in their learning				
Children are provided with experiences which meet their learning and development needs				
Children are involved in the planning of their learning process				
I receive support with my development				
I am listened to if I want to make changes to the way my room is run				
I am actively involved in the setting's self - evaluation				
I understand the settings procedure relating to safeguarding and child protection				
Any other comments				

Date :	

Building on from working in partnership with parents and staff and using the questionnaires to summarise your findings, consider doing the same for working in partnership with other settings. You can do this again anonymously either by sending out forms to the settings you work with, or by creating a Google form where you can send the link and the responses will come through.

Examples of questions:
1. How long have you been working in partnership with the setting?
2. Do we work in partnership on a regular basis?
3. Do you feel you are being listened to?
4. Do you know our safeguarding policy and procedure?
5. How does the setting provide relevant information about the needs of the children?
6. Does our setting value the contribution made by your organisation?
7. Does the setting share best practices and networking with others?
8. How does the setting work overall in partnership with yourselves?

Policies and Procedures

A policy needs to ensure that it covers the beliefs and values of your setting and show how you deliver best practice, including early years' care and education. These are standards that can suitably guide you to be able to demonstrate a professional approach and deliver best practice on a constant basis.

They need to be easily comprehended by all staff members, parents and carers. Your policies will inform your procedures and minimise risk for both children and staff within your setting. Your procedures will be formed once you have written down your policies. These are a series of actions which are carried out in a particular order.

Not only staff members, but parents and carers also need to know about the nuances of your policies and procedures. This is not a pointless exercise merely to show off to the inspector when they arrive. Policies and procedures protect yourself, your setting as well as the children.

Inspectors will need to consider a sample of policies and these will include safeguarding and child protection, risk assessments, fire safety and any other policy with relates to health and safety. This includes medicine policy and behaviour management policy.

According to The Statutory Framework of the Early Years Foundation Stage (2017) states:

'3.3. Schools are not required to have separate policies to cover EYFS requirements, provided the requirements are already met through an existing policy.

Where providers other than childminders are required to have policies and procedures as specified below, these policies and procedures should be recorded in writing.

Childminders are not required to have written policies and procedures. *However, they must be able to explain their policies and procedures to parents, carers, and others (for example Ofsted inspectors or the childminder agency with which they are registered) and ensure any assistants follow them.'*

Practice which achieves *good* to *outstanding* shows that childminders are fully aware of their policies and that these are documented in their folder and are bespoke to the childminder. I have been to many settings, including childminders, where they have thought it would be a better option to 'buy' the policies from the many sites that enable you to purchase documents which are already pre-written in order to help you in your setting. Firstly, ask yourself this…Why?

Is it to save you the effort of writing them yourself? If so, and you use them, do you understand what they mean? Consider if the wording needs to be changed to make them right for you and your practice.
This is your setting, so make sure your policies are bespoke to you and not written for anybody else. This not only helps you when you get inspected as you can always refer to the policies you have written and

understand; it also helps you take ownership of your setting.

There is nothing worse for an inspector to see these pre-written policies with no changes to show that you have reflected upon and taken ownership. You are only drawing attention to yourself, which will entail further questioning and investigation about what you know about your setting.

One of the most important policies will be your safeguarding policy and this will be asked for during your inspection.

When it comes to safeguarding children, the framework confirms
   4. 'Providers must have and implement a policy, and procedures, to safeguard children.'

This policy will be asked for during your inspection, including a sample of others. These will be checked and clarified to check you are following what it stated in your policy. If you are not following your own policy, this could lead to an *inadequate* grading.

Regarding child protection, the framework affirms the following:

'These should be in line with the guidance and procedures of the relevant Local Safeguarding Children Board (LSCB). The safeguarding policy and procedures must include an explanation of the action to be taken when there are safeguarding concerns about a child, and in the event of an allegation being made

against a member of staff, and cover the use of mobile phones and cameras in the setting.'

Your policy MUST follow your Local Safeguarding Children's Board procedure, to report any concerns and the steps that must be taken if you have an allegation against a member of your staff. It must also recommend making a time frame to do this if you have a concern or a disclosure. Usually, this is 48 hours but think back about what you had for supper two nights ago. I do not know about you, but I can't remember. So as soon as you have a concern report it to the correct authorities.

This is important, and inspectors will want to know that your Designated Safeguarding Lead is fully aware of what to do if an unforeseen situation arises.

When writing your safeguarding policy, you will realise that it is vast. Here is a list of subheadings which need to be covered. Remember, this needs to be bespoke to your setting.

a) Types of safeguarding concerns that may arise in your setting
b) How should you deal with these concerns?
c) Timeframe of raising these concerns
d) Who the designated safeguarding lead is?
e) Recruitment and supervision of staff (This does include your assistants if you are a childminder)
f) How you create a safe environment

g) How you record and store information in line with GDPR
h) How you will respond to any complaints or allegations against staff
i) Prevent duty and FGM
j) Use of mobile phones and cameras
k) E-safety

This list in not exhaustive but it does give you a fair idea on what to include.

Health

'3.45. Providers must have and implement a policy, and procedures, for administering medicines. It must include systems for obtaining information about a child's needs for medicines, and for keeping this information up-to-date. Training must be provided for staff where the administration of medicine requires medical or technical knowledge. Prescription medicines must not be administered unless they have been prescribed for a child by a doctor, dentist, nurse or pharmacist (medicines containing aspirin should only be given if prescribed by a doctor).'

Think about how you ensure that staff and parents are kept informed of your policies and procedures; when do you do this, how often do you review your policies?

Complaints

The Statutory Framework of the Early Years Foundation stage (2017) states:

3.74. 'Providers must put in place a written procedure for dealing with concerns and complaints from parents and/or carers, and must keep a written record of any complaints, and their outcome. Childminders are not required to have a written procedure for handling complaints, but they must keep a record of any complaints they receive and their outcome. All providers must investigate written complaints relating to their fulfilment of the EYFS requirements and notify complainants of the outcome of the investigation within 28 days of having received the complaint. The record of complaints must be made available to Ofsted or the relevant childminder agency on request.'

Your inspector will want to check your complaints folder to ensure that any complaints you may have had have been recorded and worked on. Any complaint needs to be reported to Ofsted so that they can also record this, regardless of how small it is. I cannot emphasise this point enough – doing so will help you show how professional you are in following your own policy to the inspector.

Policy sharing

Firstly, staff should be aware of your policies through the robust processes being followed by you. For more information, read the earlier paragraph within this chapter. You need to ensure that staff members are kept up to date with any amendments being made to your policies.

As a previous group manager, it was extremely difficult to guarantee that ALL staff members were aware of these changes. One idea we had as an *outstanding* setting was that we used to place a new policy on the back of the toilet door. Staff informed us that this was a good way of reading the policies and even though this seemed odd... the impact of reading policies this way worked!

Staff meetings were also another way of making sure that every member was kept up to date and signed to certify that they understood the new changes. This is also a good way of sharing good practice and ensuring that all staff members understood the changes and how they were going to be implemented. How do you make sure ALL staff members are aware of these changes if they do not attend staff meetings? Again, this is something that an inspector will ask staff during the day of inspection.

Writing policies

It is an excellent idea to get your entire staff involved in writing your policies; this is another way of evaluating and embedding your practice. This should not only include staff, but also your committee members if you have a committee run pre-school.

During my time in early years, I have written more policies than I care to mention. I always dreaded the time when a new version or new legislation came into play, and I had to write yet another one adding to the vast 50 we had!

As time went by, it became easier as the use of a format started to materialise. The list is immense and here are a few examples:

- Accident and incident policy
- Admissions policy
- Behaviour management policy
- Biting policy
- Compliment and complaints policy
- Equal opportunities policy
- Healthy eating policy
- Lost or missing child policy
- Non-collection of child policy
- Risk assessment policy
- Safeguarding children policy
- Settling in policy
- Trip policy
- Whistleblowing policy

These documents are very important as they will help you run your setting effectively and show to the inspector you have a good understanding on how your business runs. Again make sure they are unique to your setting.

Training and Qualifications

The inspector will want to check what training you and your staff have attended and what IMPACT (there is that word again!) it has had on your setting and the children.

We know training staff can be a problematic issue with lack of money, time out of the setting and finding the right course to meet the needs of staff members. You should be able have the documentation about the needs of your staff through the supervision and appraisal process that you have been following. Their use can help you find the right course and prove that you trying to upskill your workforce in order to make a difference within your setting.

If you are a childminder and have assistants, this also applies to them. As their manager, you need to show the inspector that you value them as an employee and are actively encouraging new knowledge and skills in your setting.

The statutory framework (2017) states:

Staff qualifications, training, support and skills
3.20. 'The daily experience of children in early years settings and the overall quality of provision depends on all practitioners having appropriate qualifications, training, skills and knowledge and a clear understanding of their roles and responsibilities.
Providers must ensure that all staff receive induction training to help them understand their roles and responsibilities. Induction training must include information about emergency evacuation procedures, safeguarding, child protection, and health and safety issues.'

'Providers must support staff to undertake appropriate training and professional development opportunities to ensure they offer quality learning and development experiences for children that continually improves.'

'Childminders are accountable for the quality of the work of any assistants, and must be satisfied that assistants are competent in the areas of work they undertake.'

This reporting requirement and documentation is needed to demonstrate that your staff members are constantly improving on their skills. How do you do that?

Part of the inspection process will be to assess the impact training has had on your setting, staff and children.

Inspectors will want to see staff continuous professional development folder and ask

- What was the last training that was attended, and what you did when you returned?
- Did you do anything with the new information you were given?
- Do staff members complete a training evaluation sheet share with the rest of your staff team?
- Do you share information at your staff meeting so that everyone who was unable to attend can get an insight to what was learned?

What is the point of this I hear you say?

Firstly, think about how each staff member has their own learning journey, just like your children do. You observe, assess and plan for children. Here's something that must be carefully noted: training is exactly the same for staff members.

- You observe staff in your setting on a day to day level
- You assess where they are in their understanding
- You plan to help them improve – hence the new training.

Remember that training is not just a tick box exercise. You need to make sure that you are improving your knowledge base and this is not only through attending face to face training.
There are many other ways in which you can do this.
- Reading a book
- E-learning
- Reading blogs or journals
- Attending other settings and sharing best practice.

One thing which need to be reiterated in that we also can improve on our practice.

Think back to this.
Do you ever get days where you observe staff and think that they have lost their way a bit? They seem to

have lost their mojo and this is impacting the delivery of children's learning.

Have you ever felt that way yourself?

Ask yourself this: When was the last time you had FIRE IN YOUR BELLY?

Collins Dictionary states that 'If you say that someone has fire in their belly, you are expressing approval of them because they are energetic, enthusiastic, and have very strong feelings.'

- When was the last time you had that?
- What made you have those feelings of being energetic and excited to share, learn and influence more?
- Do you still have those feelings now? If not, why not?
- What do you feel you need to get it back again? Is it motivation?
  Is it time? Is it training?
- Or is it all of the above?

Training and continuous development is another non-negotiable reporting requirement. Inspectors need to explore how you are ensuring you are upskilling and making consistent improvement.

The childminder continually strives for improvement and attends many relevant and childcare courses to further develop her already excellent skills. For example, following a course in the different ways children learn, she implemented specific resources to support children's individual learning styles even further.'

Maimun Khan, Childminder, Southampton

The findings of the Nutbrown review in 2012 helped with the understanding of how important upskilling and is our continual professional development. It stated:

Good quality CPD enables existing practitioners to build on their knowledge and skills, and to keep up to date with relevant research, practices and initiatives, including learning from examples in other countries. Practitioners who undertake regular CPD show a proper respect for the children and families they work with, taking a professional pride in their work, and demonstrating an understanding of their responsibility to constantly improve their practice and enhance the experience they are able to offer young children.

This is extremely important in Early Years as it is continually shown to our staff, parents, committee members as well as our inspector that we are a workforce that needs to be valued, nurtured and trained. One of the findings of the Nutbrown review was that over half of the settings who responded stated that the range and qualifications of the training did not meet the needs of their staff.

72% identified that the cost of training and covering staff members attending the training put a huge strain on their financial status, which then prevented the staff from attending this course.

Nutbrown (2012) emphasised the importance of setting accessing courses to grow their workforce; this should be evidenced during the OfSTED inspection. This is now written in the Common Inspection framework and inspectors will talk to staff members who have attended training and asked what IMPACT this has had on their setting, the children and the staff.

Thinking back to the chapter on self-evaluation, remember WHAT, SO WHAT and NOW WHAT? What was the point of the training? Are you able to demonstrate the evidence of the impact of training on you and your setting? How are you able to show this?

Qualifications

A couple of years ago, the Department for Education (2014) stated that staff who were level 3 qualified after 2014 needed to have Maths and English GCSE graded C or above so as to be included in the ratio. This had a huge impact on the numbers of Early Years educators who entered the workforce. College numbers decreased due to only enrolling students on the course if they had the relevant GCSE's. The recruitment crisis was so overwhelming that it had a knock on affect to college classes and enrolment.

From April 2017, with the new inspection framework, the changes were made due to the responses of consultation to enable staff qualifying at level 3 Early Years Educator to count in staff : child ratios with any suitable English and Maths qualifications, including functional skills as well as GCSE'S. The Government's decision to reinstate functional skills is now encouraging recruitment in colleges as well as apprenticeships.

Your inspector will want to see copies of your staff's qualification and will record this as part of their evidence for your report.

Ratios
According to the EYFS (2017), for children aged below the age of two:
- there must be at least 1 member of staff for every 3 children
- at least 1 member of staff must hold a full and relevant level 3 qualification, and must be suitably experienced in working with children under two (think how you can demonstrate this- training, past employment
- at least half of all other staff must hold a full and relevant level 2 qualification
- at least half of all staff must have received training that specifically addresses the care of babies
- in cases where there is an under two-year-olds' room, the member of staff in charge of that room must, as per the judgement of the provider, have suitable experience of working with children below the age of two.

This will need to be evidenced in the report that your inspector is writing while they are at your setting.

For children aged two:

- there must be at least 1 staff member for every four children
- at least 1 staff member must hold a full and relevant level 3 qualification
- at least half of all other staff members must hold a full and relevant level 2 qualification

For children aged three and above in registered early years provision where a person with Qualified Teacher Status, Early Years Professional Status, Early Years Teacher Status or another suitable level 6 qualification is working directly with the children,

- there must be at least one staff member for every 13 children
- at least one other staff member must hold a full and relevant level 3 qualification

For children aged three and above at any time in registered early years provision when a person with Qualified Teacher Status, Early Years Professional Status, Early Years Teacher Status or another suitable level 6 qualification is not working directly with the children,

- there must be at least 1 staff member for every 8 children
- at least 1 staff member must hold a full and relevant level 3 qualification
- at least half of all other staff members must hold a full and relevant level 2 qualification

Only staff members aged 17 or above may be included in the ratios.

Do you have volunteers in your setting?
Do you know if you can include them in your ratios?
Students who are on long term placements and volunteers (aged 17 or above) and apprentices (aged 16 or above) working towards a qualification may be included in the ratios as long as you are satisfied that they are competent and responsible. You must be able to ensure you know how you can demonstrate this.

First Aid

Much ambiguity seems to exist when it comes to First Aid and the use of such training in settings. This section will give you further clarity into what is needed to ensure you are meeting the needs of the Statutory Framework.

To be compliant with OfSTED Early Years Foundation Stage (EYFS) requirements, you need to be able to show staff members who have attended first aid training that this an appropriate, recognisable organisation approved by HSE and Ofsted.

The training should cover the following:
1. Training needs to be designed for workers caring for young children in the absence of their parents and is appropriate for the age of the children being cared for.
2. Following training, an assessment of competence needs to lead to an award of a certificate.
3. This certificate must be renewed every three years.

With regard to the EYFS and Ofsted requirements, you should have at least one 12 hour full paediatric first aid qualified staff member available at all times, including cover for sickness, holidays and trips. The 12 hour paediatric first aid trained staff can be supported by one day Emergency Paediatric First Aid trained staff.

This must be renewed every three years. Ensure that if your staff members and children are having trips. One staff member must be first aid trained using a first aid kit when they are out with children. As well as on a trip or outing you will need to take into account the number of children, staff and layout of your setting to ensure that a paediatric first aider is able to respond to emergencies expeditiously.

All newly qualified staff to the early years workforce who have completed a level 2 and/or level 3 qualification on or after **30 June 2016** MUST also have either a full PFA or an emergency PFA certificate within **three** months of commencing work in order to be included in the required staff: child ratios at level 2 or level 3 in an Early Years setting·

Your inspector will check this during the day of inspection and would want to see those certificates, which ideally should be on display or made available to parents if needed.

Please be mindful if you have these on display, you are in accordance of GDPR regulations and have asked staff permission for this.

As evidenced from this chapter, training and qualification is highly important to ensure that you are delivering high quality learning to children and that the IMPACT this has on their development is positive and long lasting. One thing to remember is to reflect on your learning process and think about how it is likely to impact your role as a teacher or role in the future.

While there is no one size fits all, no matter where you are in your career or learning, these pointers will hold you in good stead and play a constructive role in helping you attain *outstanding*.

Example Training evaluation form

What did I attend and when?
In the moment planning June 2018

Why did I attend the course?
The setting wants to implement a new way of planning with ideas and interest from children.

What did I learn?
I learnt that we need to be focusing not only on teaching, but also on how well we know about children, the use of our environment and the questioning techniques we have as practitioners

How am I going to implement this into my setting?
Through our staff team meetings, I will deliver an 'in the moment' planning question and answer session. I will use the staff's knowledge and expertise to better understand children's interests and ensure we are working with parents in order to understand a better way of informing us about children's ever changing development.

How will I know what IMPACT it has had on my setting?
Children's learning will be at the forefront of our planning and all assessments will be ongoing. Staff members will have a deeper understanding of what the children's next steps are and not have to keep revisiting the tapestry. Children's assessment and planning will be at the heart of the setting and we

> will be able to produce evidence of what we are
> doing to meet the needs of individual children.

Throughout the whole leadership and management
chapter you will have realised that evaluating your
practice is of high priority. Ensure this approach is
constant as this is part of your own reflection of your
setting and practice.

During the inspection process you will also be
expected to have a leadership and management
discussion with the inspector. With this in mind we
have created a list of questions which may help you
with making sure you are fully aware and in
preparation for this time.

1. How do you make sure staff are gaining more
    knowledge and improving their skills?
    How often do you have supervisions and
    appraisals?

2. How does the staff get involved with these?

3. What is the induction process?

4. What is your DBS process?

5. How do you cascade information to staff?

6. What do you understand about Prevent Duty?

7. If I were to ask a member of staff about
    prevent duty would they know what it meant?

(The inspector will also speak to staff member)

8. If you had concerns who would you speak to?

9. What do you staff know about British Values and how are these used in the setting?

10. Who is the Lead Safeguarding officer?

6. TEACHING, LEARNING AND ASSESSMENT

Throughout this chapter, we will focus on what your inspector will want to see and what they will do to make sure you are having an impact on children' s learning through your teaching.

Throughout the day, the inspector would judge the effectiveness of your teaching, learning and assessment by process evaluating the extent to which:

a) You are able to show what a child is able to achieve in your setting. This must also include children who are not exceeding or exceeding in their development. If they are exceeding, your inspector will want to see that you are continually demonstrating that the child is making progress and that you are working proactively to ensure that they do not fall behind in their development.

b) You are able to show to the inspector that you understand the age group you are working with, and are able to demonstrate this within your teaching and assessments.

c) Baseline assessments are taken from when a child starts, which includes parents' views and other providers such as preschools, childminders and day nurseries the child may have attended.

d) The assessments you are writing on the child are used to plan for the next stage of learning; this is able to identify children who need extra support in order to help them do well.

e) You are able to show how you interact and encourage children to facilitate their development using questioning and critically thinking.

f) You are able to show how parents understand how their children are progressing and how they can contribute and support their child's learning.

g) You are able to show you are recognising diversity and equality of opportunity is being encouraged throughout all learning and teaching

h) You are able to prove that the teaching you are incorporating helps children secure skills and develop/learn successfully. This will ensure they are able to be ready for school.

Throughout the day, the Early Years inspector will want to see how effective your teaching is to ensure that children are developing using the characteristics of effective learning.

The key evidence that you will need to show is how well children are:

- Playing and exploring
- Being active in their learning
- Being able to think critically and creating

You will need to show how you evaluate your teaching to support children's learning and ensure that you are aware of the stages and ages of your children in your setting.

'Children's learning is meticulously planned and is informed by the regular and precise assessments of their development. Staff constantly reshape activities to help children to develop their concentration skills and to motivate them to keep trying. Staff are skilled and confident in knowing when to allow time for children to lead their own learning.'

Little Learners, Corby

Your inspector will want to observe how children interact with each other, including with you and your staff, as well as how this will impact their progress. Evidence will be gathered on the progress of different groups of children and how these are recorded. For example, age cohorts, boys versus girls and children with English as an additional language.

This does include the Progress check at 2, parent contributions and also the summative reports which are shared when children leave for school. From your assessment in your setting, the inspector will want to see that you are able to plan effectively and encouraging the traits of effective learning.

They will also want to see the impact of your staff's qualification, knowledge, training along with their own learning and development. The quality of all activities in each age group will be considered on the basis of their efficacy.

Through the day, the inspector will want to observe children's learning and the way staff members interact with children throughout each of those activities.

This chapter will explore the understanding each of the following:

- Teaching
- Learning
- Assessment

This is to give you a better understanding of what is to be expected during the inspection process.

Things to remember during your inspection day:

OfSTED (2017) state in their outstanding descriptors

Practitioners use their expert knowledge of learning and deep understanding of how children learn to provide a rich, varied and imaginative experiences that enthuse, engage and motivate children to learn.

Use the guidance as a checklist to ensure you are meeting the Teaching, Learning and Assessment needs.

JIGSAW
Early Years Consultancy

CHILDREN'S FUTURE'S MATTER

Questions to ask yourself	Always	Some times	Never
Do you have a balance of adult-led and child-led activities?			
Are children being asked open-ended question?			
Do your staff members give children enough time to answer a question?			
Are they making eye contact when children eventually answer the question?			

How do you evaluate your activities?			
Is this being evidenced to show IMPACT?			
Are children given a choice of where, when and what they can play with?			
Can children easily access open-ended resources to enable critical thinking skills?			
Are children being encouraged to be curious and independent learners?			
Do practitioners encourage			

children's interests and include their experiences?			
Do practitioners encourage children to try out new things and learn from their mistakes?			
Are practitioners confident about observing, assessing and planning for the children's next stage of learning?			
Do practitioners encourage children to support each other to achieve a goal?			
Do practitioners know how to			

motivate children and have high expectations of them?			
Do practitioners exhibit enthusiasm and full engagement with children?			
Do practitioners model language which encourages children to think and prepare for next stage of learning?			
Do practitioners create opportunities for 'teachable moments' and record these effectively?			
Do practitioners observe the levels			

of engagement children have in their room?			
Do practitioners fully understand the needs of babies and their care routines?			

The Characteristics of Effective Teaching

Inspectors will want to see that you are effectively teaching children through the activities you include whilst also facilitating their learning.

Children cannot be accurately assessed without helping them learn successfully. They cannot successfully learn without having an effective teaching system.

I know some of you may read this and say you are not a teacher. It does not matter if you are a teacher or not, if you have early years children in your care you are teaching the skills to progress. FACT.

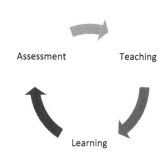

Assessment   Teaching

Learning

Take an entire day (today) to look at the activities that you are providing and setting up for your children. Taking this time will help you reflect on what you have and what you need to change.

- Do you feel you can improve upon them?
- How do you evaluate your activities and your continuous provision or your environment?
- Do you get all staff involved?
- Do you get the children involved?
- If not, again what is stopping you!

Children need to be involved with their setting. They are the ones that are learning throughout the day. If you are not questioning, facilitating, investigating, communicating with children to extend their learning, then you should be thinking:

Is this the right job for me?

Your inspector cannot show they have preferred practice when they inspect and cannot offer any advice. This was one of the areas I found hard when I was inspecting. I could give recommendations but advice throughout the day was frowned upon. Hence, Jigsaw Early Years Consultancy was born.

As long as you are showing that the things you are doing are having a positive impact on children's learning and development, you will be good.

There is much debate about how we should plan. To be able to plan 'in the moment' for children, you need to get the basics right first. The Statutory Framework for the Early Years Foundation Stage (2017) states:

The **learning and development requirements** *cover:*
- *the* **areas of learning and development** *which must shape activities and experiences (***educational programmes***) for children in all early years settings*
- *the* **early learning goals** *that providers must help children work towards (the knowledge, skills and understanding children*

should have at the end of the academic year in which they turn five)
- **assessment arrangements** *for measuring progress (and requirements for reporting to parents and/or carers)'*

The term teaching can sometimes be contrived as being a formal way of working. It covers a wide umbrella of numerous ways in which practitioners can help children learn. During some of my inspections, I have had conversations with childminders who say they are not teachers as I have briefly mentioned before, but I am afraid that this statement is not quite true. As parents, we are teachers and as practitioners we are teachers; yet, we are also are facilitators.

We facilitate children's learning and play during planned and child initiated activities. We model our language and communicate with them by demonstrating, explaining, showing, exploring, investigating, encouraging and recalling, as well as setting and extending challenges.

We need to take account of the resources we provide, the environment and surroundings, as well as the structure of the day. When thinking about the resources, we need to be able to provide a breadth of different textures, shapes, sizes and resources that are interpreted in terms of whatever a child wants them to be. It is all about the process and not the end product.

The whole point of them being open-ended is that they can become a whole new world for a child. This can be a struggle for the practitioner as they have only known what they know based on their past experience. Think about this.

Take a real apple – write down everything you can to describe the apple and questions to ask about it. When I have done this training with my delegates, the amount of questions was in the high 40's.

Now take a plastic apple – cross off any questions from your previous list which you cannot ask about the apple you now have. How many questions do you have now?

Now take a printed picture of an apple – cross off any questions which are not suitable for the picture. How many questions do you have?

This type of exercise is so important in that it encourages you to think about the resources you have in your setting. The more open-ended resources you have, the more thought provoking questions, critical thinking skills and creativity is being used by children.

Think about our brain for one second. Think of it as a muscle. Just like any other muscle, if we do not use the brain it will waste away.

This is why we need to ensure that we are providing the most effective form of teaching as possible to help children learn and develop. You are the source!

Sustained Shared thinking

A good definition of sustained shared thinking is as follows:

'Sustained shared thinking' occurs when two or more individuals 'work together' in an intellectual way to solve a problem, clarify a concept, evaluate an activity, extend a narrative etc.

Both parties must contribute to the thinking and it must develop and extend the understanding. It was more likely to occur when children were interacting 1:1 with an adult or with a single peer partner and during focussed group work.'

The Effective Provision of Pre-School Education (EPPE) Project (2004)

This gave us a better understanding of what sustained shared thinking meant and how it is so fundamental to how we use this practice as practitioners through our teaching so as to ensure that children are learning.

When a child becomes absorbed in a conversation with a practitioner or their interests are captivated during an activity, this will ignite their learning, use their brain and provoke investigation further. Children will want to discover more and with the help of you as the facilitator, the learning will begin. The story will begin to unfold and children will begin to ask questions themselves with their peers.

Whether it is one to one or with a small group, sustained shared thinking can be a powerful tool to provide a connection between all. This in turn forms a relationship where children are feeling nurtured and secure. Opportunities will arise to reveal a level of cognitive development, boosting both self-esteem and self-worth. The feeling of being valued in a child's eyes is of utmost importance. Hence, personal, social and emotional well-being is one of the prime areas. We need to get this right and then learning will begin to flow as it should.

The theories about sustained shared thinking contributed to the original EYFS, which explicitly stated that sustained shared thinking should be an integral part of a child's creativity and critical thinking (EYFS 4.3). It is also indirectly described in **all** the areas of learning and development.

When you are planning for children's activities, do you specifically look at areas they need to be developing and create activities which fit into that area of learning.

Why do you do this?

Think about your time and what you want the child to learn?

Throughout my inspections, I have seen activities being facilitated which only cover one specific area of learning. Think about how time consuming this is and what is it that the child can get from that activity. Or areas are perfectly labelled covering all areas of learning. Think about why you do this. If you do this is it for your benefit or the children? Do the children develop more with those labelled zones? If not, why do you have them?

It is not an Ofsted requirement for you to have labelled areas. If it is for rich print environments, think of other ways you can achieve this? Books, for example!

Why not try this at your next staff meeting?

Give an item to each person - only one item and see how they can link it to all areas of learning. This will not only help with observations, but will also make you and your staff think about the activities you are offering and how they can impact your children's development.

Let us take the example of a pen. Write down everything the pen can be used to promote ALL the areas of learning. I use this example in my Quality Improvement Inspections and highly recommend you do this at your staff training. Use the form below to help you with this training exercise.

This will be a good staff meeting exercise to encourage staff to think outside the box. The more this is done, the more practitioners will be aware that everything we give a child can encompass all areas of learning.

Things to remember during your inspection day:

OfSTED (2017) stated in their outstanding descriptors:

'Practitioners use their expert knowledge of learning and deep understanding of how children learn to provide a rich, varied and imaginative experiences that enthuse, engage and motivate children to learn.'

Think about the following when you are preparing for your inspection.

- Have you planned for all seven areas of learning?
- How are you developing your practitioners to become experts in children's development and learning?
- How do you ensure that the environment is suitable for the age of the child?
- How do you ensure that children are engaged consistently?

Inspectors will want to see how you evaluate your teaching in your own setting.

Do you perform peer on peer observations?

I would highly recommend that you start performing peer on peer observations if you haven't already. This will not only help when you are eventually observed, but will also go a long way in ensuring that you are evaluating your staff practice and making recommendations to improve.

In order to make peer observations successful, all practitioners need to be fully involved and be willing to reflect on their own practice. The practitioner does need to have a responsibility to take constructive feedback once the observation is complete. Feedback needs to be given when there are no children around and an ideal way would be to link with staff supervisions. (See Chapter 1)

Peer observations should be able to

- Acknowledge your skills, celebrate strengths and recognise your knowledge
- Encourage you to identify areas for your continuous professional development
- Give you accountability to improve your practice
- Empower you new ways of working
- Develop a professional relationship with your peers. (I would highly recommend you to perform peer observations on each other if you are a childminder; this is exceptional practice)
- Enable you to upskill your practice
- Use the information as part of your supervision process
- Provide reflective evidence for Ofsted and your setting's Self-Evaluation

See example below

JIGSAW

PEER on PEER OBSERVATION FORM

Observer:		Practitioner Observed:	
Room:	Date	Time:	
Focus of the Observation:			
Does the practitioner do any of the following?			
Use simple repetitive language during the activity	Yes/No	Use vocabulary that the children can understand in everyday instructions	Yes/No
Gain children's attention before delivering instructions	Yes/No	Give children time to respond	Yes/No
Talk at an appropriate rate using short sentences	Yes/No	Use natural gesture and facial expression to support language	Yes/No
Adapt their language to the level of the child	Yes/No	Use some simple signs to communicate with children who are struggling with some language	Yes/No
Model the correct sentence when they hear a child's incorrect utterance	Yes/No	Speaking sensitively to shy or unsettled children.	Yes/No
Encourage the children to ask questions	Yes/No	Encouraging children's independence and self-confidence by acknowledging all efforts.	Yes/No
Facilitating shared play and turn taking.	Yes/No	Modelling activities and talking about what the child is doing	Yes/No
Modelling a range of positive behaviour and language	Yes/No	Using questions that invite conversation or encourage reasoning rather than yes or no answers	Yes/No
Responding positively to children's efforts to communicate	Yes/No	Actively supporting children in solving their problems and disputes	Yes/No
What were the strengths?			
Action Plan after the observation			
Targets you have set yourself / areas for your own development: * * *			
Signed by Observer: Signed by practitioner:			

Now we have finished focusing on your teaching practice, let us move on to the way children learn.

Learning

Inspectors will ensure that they are able to acquire evidence the following Characteristics of Effective Learning through the characteristics of effective teaching. This is the paramount to a child's journey within your setting.

They will want to see that children are able to play and explore their surroundings, be active in their learning and are able to think critically and be creative. Children's outcomes will be met through the art of your effective teaching. The impact of your teaching will ensure that you have a secure understanding of children's learning. Through the quality of your activities, you will be able to show that children's development is paramount to every day practice.

We know that teaching, learning and assessment is collectively referred to as the observation, assessment and planning cycle. But how effective is this in your setting? The strands need to link to each other in order to show a tangible IMPACT on children's learning. We cannot effectively do one without the other.

It is a bit like a Jigsaw puzzle.

You can have all these pieces placed on your table, but it's what do you do with them that will eventually matter.

Do you put the pieces around the outside and then start completing in the middle to make the picture? Or do you randomly take a piece and try to find another that will fit with the one which is in your hand?

Like a puzzle, you need to have a method to implement your plan.

Can you honestly say that you do all three aspects of this cycle effectively and are able to maximize impact within your setting? Are you able to show how effectively children are learning through your successful teaching? This needs to be constant throughout your setting in each age group to have any chance of achieving good or outstanding.

Through the many inspections I have been a part of as an Early Years Inspector and then as a consultant through our Quality Improvement Inspections, I have noticed that the three areas do not always work in conjunction with each other. This then shows that the impact of what you are teaching is not being reflected in the children's learning and within the assessments you are writing. Again, if you are not showing any impact this will affect your overall grade.

If you are not able to show how effectively and consistently you are demonstrating impacting think why is that?
What do you think is the reason for this?

- Is it a time issue?
- Is it a training issue?
- Is it a monitoring issue?

Or is it all three?

We need to ensure that our practice is reflective and realise that we can improve upon how we deliver to ensure the children's needs are being met constantly.

There are four overarching principles which are able to shape our best practices.

- Unique Child
- Positive relationships
- Enabling Environment
- Children develop and learn in different ways and at different rates

As well as the four principles and getting the basics right you also need to make sure that you are covering **all** of the 7 areas of the Early Years Foundation Stage

Prime areas
Personal, social and emotional
Physical development

Communication and Language

Specific Areas
Literacy
Mathematics
Understanding the World
Expressive Arts and Design

So, let us go back to the basics and talk about the most important –
the UNIQUE child.

The understanding of the principles of EYFS is paramount in understanding how a child learns best. There are many approaches we can follow which helps us with best practice, but it is highly important for us to understand that we cannot do these approaches without taking into account the needs of our children. Each child in your setting is unique. They all have different learning styles, and their needs are different from each other. They also have different interests and develop in different ways. We need to take into account this first before planning our children's learning journey to ensure that we have covered the bare necessities.

Take the time now to reflect upon each child. Use one week to not observe, assess or plan for the children in your care; instead, take a step back and follow where they go.

- Do they have a particular interest in an area of your setting?

- Do they have a schema?
- Do they prefer to be hands on or just sit back and watch?
- Do they like to get their hands dirty or do they prefer not to partake in your creative activities you have set out?
- Do you need to set out activities, or are children able to choose for themselves and encourage their peers to be involved in their play?

This activity is very important to get to know your children and I highly recommend this happens when you have new children starting with you. Observe their cycle of learning and make notes. This will help you plan for them eventually and knowing their style can help you out when your inspector asks you to explain about a particular key child. They will want you to tell them everything and demonstrate that you understand their learning journey.

Use the time this week to extensively focus on this.

Just one week.
It will not make *any* difference to your assessments of your children; in fact it will have a positive IMPACT on their learning as you are being secure in your understanding of them as a child.

Carry post it notes and make intelligent notes of your key child's interests. This will give you a found basis of knowing what unique means to children within your setting. Use this information to start being the facilitator in the children's story of their time with you.

Once you have the information, Observe and Record after one week.

Use the first observation after this week as a baseline for where you think your children are. We will discuss this further on in the understanding of assessments.

Positive relationships

Your inspector will want to analyse the relationship you have with children within your setting.

Positive relationships that are formed between staff and children are able to give children a feeling of belonging and sense of self-worth. Relationships need to be warm and loving; the practitioner needs to be very sensitive to a child's needs. They are encouraging, supportive and consistent with their boundaries. These relationships are a clear way of providing stimulating conversations wherein the practitioner becomes a facilitator for the child's needs.

The inspector will want to talk to the children's key person and ask them to talk about a particular child they are observing. They will want the practitioner to know the child's interests, where they currently are in their stages of learning, and what their next steps are. They will also want to observe these steps being worked upon to show that they are making an impact in a child's learning.

The Early Years Foundation Stage (2017) explains that practitioners would do well to be sensitive to a child's needs and respond sensitively to extend their learning and curiosity. By a practitioner observing and tuning in to a child, they will be able to discover what they like to do, when they are confident in their surroundings and when they are in need of extra guidance.

Effective learning can only be demonstrated when children are being motivated; they will begin to show signs of concentrations and will engage in meaningful play where they are able to use their critical thinking skills, learn from their mistakes and become resilient.

Equally, effective learning can only be determined when practitioners are able to model active listening skills. To that end, the use of eye contact and responses to a child's discoveries begin to have significance.

Think back to when asking a question to a child. How long did you wait for an answer?

Giving children adequate time to answer a question not only ensures that they have a feeling of self-worth, but also encourages their brain to respond more effectively to the question. If you keep asking questions, children will tend to remember the last word you shared with them. Practitioners need to show respect to children and let them learn for themselves in their own unique way.

It is often said that environment is the third teacher. This idea was postulated by the schools of Reggio Emilia, who opined that the experiences that children are learning within your environment hold the key to any successful development. Providing resources for children to participate and collaborate with their peers whilst also being facilitated by the practitioner is paramount to embedding learning in a child's day.

Think about your environment and take a glance at areas where children are actively learning. The use of observations will be immensely helpful to evaluate how your children are learning, and which areas are being enthusiastically used and constantly developed by children within their own play and learning. Open-ended resources are highly effective in a child's day and need to be actively promoted. Encouraging children to use curiosity in order to develop their own critical thinking and skills provides the basis of vital learning.

Generally, children are born curious and the one thing we all know that in today's society, personal, social and emotional development is high on the agenda of any learning. In order to become curious, children need to explore the world around them, and an open-ended environment gives them just that. It has no pre-determined boundaries and there is no fixed outcome. Children are also able to follow their own imagination and enable their creativity to take them wherever they want to go. Indisputably, this is paramount for learning to take place.

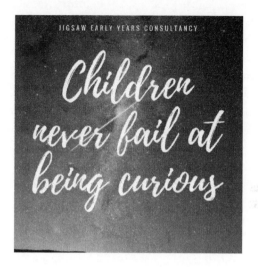

Children learn best through provocations which you provide for them. Over the past year, the word provocations have been spreading like wildfire.

Do you know what this means?

Firstly, the term originated from the Reggio approach. Put simply, provocations means provoking learning by enticing children to play and encouraging them to be curious and creative; all characteristics of Effective Learning which we need to aim toward and ensure become known to us within our children's everyday learning.

Now, it is tempting to think that you do this day in and day out by making your setting inviting and enabling children to share their interests; however, these resources need to open ended so that children can decide what they want to do, how they want to do it and when they want to do it. Remember, children learn more during a process rather than an end product. However lovely it may be, children need to feel their learning is being valued through their own processes.

Are we being too adult led? Again, another debatable question. But the fact is that children learn best when they are interested in what they want to do, not by what you want them to do!

In The Art of Thought, Wallas (1926) suggests that we have 4 processes

- **Preparation**
- **Simmering/ incubation**
- **Illumination**
- **Verification**

Preparation – when we are being creative, we investigate all areas.

Simmering/ incubation – creativity can drift towards two ways - positive and negative - and it's up to the artist to find helpful solutions by using our brain.

Illumination – after the above two stages, the A-ha or Eureka moment eventually occurs.

Verification – is in the creating the creation!

Linking to provocations, we should be making sure that our activities are interesting and original to the child. They need to find the direction they want to go towards to make it their original learning. That's what it's all about- keeping it simple.

Try it. Visit your local scrap store and place the resources around your setting. Sit back and watch what happens… Think about what Wallas suggests. The art lies in provoking communication and language to get children to think for themselves!

Your inspector will not want be able to take into account the different approaches or ethos you have in your setting, but they do need to see what a child is learning within your setting.

Think about this.

You can use two tinned cans.

Can 1: Is labelled stating what is inside of it (tomato soup, in this exercise).

Can 2: There is no label. It is a plain silver tinned can.

Which one of the above is going to provoke more curiosity, creativity, critical thinking skills, investigations, discovery and exploration?

The next time you set activities out for children, use these questions as a tool for you staff?

- What area of learning are children achieving with this activity?
- What skills will children be using?
- Will this engage and excite children?
- Will this provoke imagination and spark inspiration?
- Will this be a good basis for children to take the activity off to something new?

The involvement in children's learning assumes topmost priority for them to learn. Indicators of such involvement give us vital clues of how children are learning. It is a process which starts at a very young age – from the time they are babies - where connections to the brain grow and join together to form other connections. Without this, children will not develop. Emotions, regardless of whether they are positive or negative, have an impact on the way children learn. Negative emotions will not encourage synapse to join and create stress & anxiety in a child's life, which adversely impacts their learning whereas positive experiences in a child life will give them the desired hunger to learn more and ensure that their own life's trajectory is moving forward.

Children have an eagerness to learn and be curious. They delight in being investigators and are able to discover new ways of learning. It is all about the process they are learning and not merely the product they are aiming for.
I have been to several inspections where I see end products of what children have created.

Think about this!

Have children produced the Mothers or Father's day card? What impact did this have on their learning? Why did we do these activities?

Children need to be able to process what they are doing, and this can only be done by being unique in their own learning. Worksheets are another example of a product of something which the children have not been the original supplier.

Pieces of artwork should be from a child's own perspective and not from ours. It should not be because parents want to see this end result. When you show parents around if you explained to them why each piece of artwork will be individual, this will surely show you are treating each child as their own. Again, they are UNIQUE.

The point of process over product is that there is no right or wrong way. There are no step by step instructions or samples for children to follow. They are able to show their own meanings and there is not right or wrong way to explore or create. The pieces of art that are produced remain highly focused on the child's experiences and exploration of tools, material and media.

The whole process will be calm and children will spend much longer creating their own masterpieces. It will be the child's choice. Your inspector will want to see how you are encouraging this type of learning. They will also want to observe children making choices and be confident within their surroundings. They will want to see practitioners to facilitate this style of learning and be able to share their findings with the inspector.

English as an Additional Language

Children who have English as an additional language is currently a hot topic and your inspector will want to see what opportunities children have to develop and be able to use their home language during their play and learning, whilst also supporting their language at home.

Language used in a child's own home needs to be developed in your setting within their learning and development. Much research from Chomsky explains that children learn from their home language early on and are able to extend this learning during their early years.

On this basis, what are we scared of when there are children who start in our setting? Is it because we are scared of getting it wrong or not knowing what to say?

During an inspection I visited early on in my inspection experience, I was able to observe a child enter the pre-school and just wander around. I chose this child as I clearly fathom that he was nervous and zoomed straight to the sand pit.

I observed and I recorded for two hours. During that time he did not move from the sand pit; he did not play with the sand, nor did he build anything. His hands were just placed within the sand and he was gazing around the room.

This child did not has English as his first language.

When I had finally stopped evidencing what I was seeing, I requested to speak to his key person. They did not know the child's next steps or where they were in their areas of learning. I inevitably got concerned about him. I explained that I had been observing this child for a lengthy period of time and did not find anyone talking to him.
The practitioner looked at me and said she did not know what to say to him as he did not speak English.

Are your eyebrows as raised as mine as I am writing this?

So, not only did the setting know this child had English as a second language; they also did not know what his next steps were as observations were not neither accurate nor recorded effectively to show where he was in his learning.

I asked how they would have felt if no-one spoke to them for two hours. If not one person acknowledged their presence, how would that make them feel? The limited communication and language support for this child surely did not prepare him for school where he was supposed to go to within the next few months. Interactions from the staff remained poor and also showed that the opportunities of learning and engaging in worthwhile activities were limited.

Needless to say, this setting did not achieve a positive grading.

Children's home language is very important to provide those critical family links, especially if you have children who are being cared for by older, non-English speaking family members. Between the children and their carers - they need to be able to have purposeful conversations with each other.

Assessment

Throughout the day, the inspector will want to see how you are analysing and reviewing children's learning based on what you have observed. You need to see what has taken place throughout a variety of processes such as examples of children's work through mark making, evidence from any photographs you may have taken, and discussions from parents about things you have not observed before.

Your inspector will want to see where a child was when they started with you.

This is referred to as starting points or Baseline assessments.

Whenever I have visited settings and asked to see the children's starting points, there has been no consistency about when these were written. It constitutes a good practice to enable a child settle in your setting before you set out to track a child; however, you can observe visually from day 1 and a highly efficient practitioner will begin to build a picture of the child during this time. They will also start to see a child's likes and dislikes whilst analysing the way they are learning. This in turn will ensure that children's unique ways are being taken into consideration during their development.

As part of this process we need to gain information from parents also as part of the starting points' process. How do you do this in your setting? As mentioned previously, parents are the first educator and gaining this information is paramount to working in partnership. The information gathered when a child starts with can be a good way of gathering much useful information. Using 'All about me' documents as part of the settling in time and gathering at home visits begins to set up a clear picture of a child.

This is such an important time to tell parents how often you will be observing and assessing their children - and how important it is for them to contribute. On their part, parents will want to know who their child's key person is; this will start to form the much-needed relationship in Early Years settings.

It is also a good practice to ensure that you are meeting the needs of a child and that their starting points are assessed within the first three weeks maximum. This will give you adequate time to take parental contributions into consideration. Using the areas of learning, the key person should be able to make a judgement from their observations to decipher where a child is working within and identify the stages of learning and development through a 'best fit' judgement.

Use the headings

- Beginning
- Developing
- Secure

These will help you prepare the first chapter of a child's journey and ensure that you are meeting their particular needs.

Exceptional practice would be necessary to make sure this is consistent within your setting. Think about how can you demonstrate this?

If you are a day nursery, one way that I recommend within my own Quality Improvement Inspections is to complete a Starting point or Baseline assessment at the point of entry to each room. This will not only ensure that children's assessments are kept up to date, but also prove that practitioners are consistent in applying their knowledge of children's development.

Use this baseline form to find out where your children are at their starting points.

JIGSAW

Baseline assessment
Key

| B - Beginning | D - Developing | S - Secure |

Name of child:																			
Date of birth:		0-11 months			8-20 months			16-26 months			22-36 months			30-50 months			40-60+ months		
Prime Areas of Learning		B	D	S	B	D	S	B	D	S	B	D	S	B	D	S	B	D	S
Personal, Social and Emotional Development	Making relationships																		
	Self-confidence and Self-awareness																		
	Managing feelings and behaviour																		
Communication and Language	Listening and Attention																		
	Understanding																		
	Speaking																		
Physical Development	Moving and Handling																		
	Health and Self-care																		
Specific Areas of Learning		B	D	S	B	D	S	B	D	S	B	D	S	B	D	S	B	D	S
Literacy	Reading																		
	Writing	*	*	*	*	*	*	*	*	*									
Mathematics	Numbers																		
	Shape, space and measures	*	*	*															
Understanding the World	People and Communities	*	*	*	*	*	*												
	The World																		
	Technology	*	*	*	*	*	*												
Expressive Arts and Design	Exploring and using media and materials	*	*	*															
	Being imaginative	*	*	*	*	*	*												

Through the art of consistent observations over a period of time, children's own learning story will start to evolve and with the use of your provocations, invitations and facilitating their play progress will be made and next steps can be planned for. This is called the assessment of learning and is based on the information you have to inform your everyday planning. It is also called formative assessment.

The other form of assessments is called summative assessment. This is written by summarising the evidence you have collated from the formative assessments over a period of time and condensing the information to share with parents and outside agencies so as to show the progress children have made.

If you do these, think about when you write these at this particular time.

The inspector will want to see how you do this and its impact on the children's own learning journey.

Providing this type of assessment is paramount when working in partnership with parents as this gives them a guide of which stage their child is currently in and how they can help ensure that they are developing, or if any interventions need to take place.

A good idea to share summative assessments is at the end of each term. If practitioners start to give evidence of their understanding of where a child is currently situated, then this will show that they have a good knowledge on how to develop and provide the requisite tools for the next stage of learning.

Jigsaw has an example of these forms. To obtain a copy please go to our website www.jigsawearlyyearsconsultnancy.com and request the form.

It is important to show how you provide evidence on children's progression to the inspector. One practical method of showing this would be is through cohort tracking. It is really important that you understand what this means and entails given that it will impact the judgement of your setting.

Cohort tracking is used to show where a particular group of children are in their assessments while in your setting. For example, a group could be between boys and girls, the cohort of children starting school, or children who have EYPP (Early Years Pupil Premium). Children who are making less that typical progress must be identified and shown to your inspector to demonstrate how you are going to reduce the differences.

Inspectors will want to see their starting points as well as the progress they are making. The evidence you have must ensure that you are aware of any additional needs and how you are going to ensure these do not have any impact on a child's learning journey.

The Early Years Inspection Handbook (2017) states:

'Monitoring ensures that individual children or groups of children who have identified needs are targeted and appropriate interventions are secured so that children receive the support they need, including through effective partnerships with external agencies and other providers.'

This is a reporting requirement and as a setting you need to show you are intervening when possible through the needs you have identified.

The whole objective of showing different cohorts of children is to highlight learning needs of groups of children and individuals, to be able to identify the next steps to inform your future planning, and to provide information to parents and ensure that teaching is successful to impact on what children are learning and support good practice.

After reading this you are probably thinking that it is all about the paperwork. This is not true. Yes, you need to show you are recording and evidencing where children are but the cohort tracker is paramount to ensure you are monitoring children's progress. Good practice would be to encourage practitioners in their own rooms to do a cohort tracker. Not only will this ensure you are all singing from the same hymn sheet; this is also a way of ensuring staff are feeling valued and being part of the bigger picture.

Analysing each cohort tracker is vital to ensure every child is getting the support they need and to identify if a child is showing signs of delay in an area of development. It highlights each child's individual needs and ensures this is being planned for with appropriate activities that are challenging and for children to achieve. Your inspector will want to see how each child is being supported and how these needs are met. By demonstrating to your inspector your cohort tracker you are verifying that you have identified these needs and your action plan to ensure that the differences between children are being reduced.

Cohort tracker ideally should be completed every term after the summative assessments have been written. These will then inform where a child is and any gaps that need to be narrowed. It is at this time where, as a previous inspector, I have seen managers of settings relying on staff to accurately assess children in the seven areas of learning.

Think about the process.

- How do you ensure practitioners are monitoring children effectively?
- Do you have a process in place which can evidence that you are tracking your staff's observations on children, or do you rely on staff to do this and trust what they are doing?

It is highly important to make sure the job of tracking is effective.
Think about the observation cycle and the Jigsaw pieces we were discussing earlier. You cannot have one without the other.

Tips to provide an effective cohort tracker

- Use observations to support your tracking and ensure staff are knowledgeable in children's development to understand where they are.
- Ensure you monitor staff observations and assessments are coherent and consistent.
- Use the cohort tracker to identify any weaknesses between the groups of children such as boys and girls, children with additional needs, children with English as a second language, disadvantaged children.
- Use this information to set targets on how to improve where a child is. Record this to demonstrate that you are doing something about it.

Whichever way you assess children, whether it is paper based or using online journals, you will need to show your inspector how confident you are in child development.

By ensuring that children are being taught inspirationally, you can ensure that they are successfully learning. Through the success of their learning you will be able to assess effectively. It's a cycle... Get this right and you are showing the impact you are making.

Tracking children

Although having an Ofsted inspection and guidance is highly important for us, as long we show what impact we are having on our children, they are not able to judge you on the way deliver practice in our setting.

You need to show that we are delivering a welcoming, nurturing and evolving practice which meets the needs and outcomes of all children who walk through your door. You need to grow as a setting and discover what works well for us and our children. You all know your children better than anyone else. Remember that. You will have a range of techniques that are suited to your learning styles of children and you need to ensure that this quality is of the highest form.

Think back... Can you honestly say this is done consistently?
Again, to achieve the outstanding grading this needs to be done continually.

By meeting the needs of all the welfare requirements and the Statutory Framework for the Early Years Foundation Stage, you are well on your way of evidencing you are meeting those needs. Once this has been achieved, you then need to look at your practice little by little to make sure this is effective for all children, and not just the ones who are exceeding.

What about children who need a little help, or the invisible child that doesn't give you a stressful day or the one who wanders around the room looking for things to do? The one who rarely engages in conversation with you unless you are asking a question... If that is the case, please make sure it's open-ended to extend their learning.

Your inspector will track two children during the day. Children with English as an additional language, or who are on Early Years pupil premium will be the one of the first children to be tracked. Use this time now before your inspection to put in place peer on peer observations - linking to the tracking of children's learning and development to show you are evaluating your practice. This not only links to Teaching Learning and Assessment, but also to leadership and management. The monitoring of children's assessment needs to be maintained and consistent to show you that being evaluative and children are making progress.

Tracking

The inspector will track the learning of two children and will sample their development journals to see where you have placed them. They will want to see the quality of the assessments and knowledge of staff about their key children. They will want to see the Progress check at two children and who this information is shared with. If you have any children who are on the Early Years pupil premium, they will want to see the impact of the funding and how you can demonstrate these children are thriving in your care.

If you are a childminder, they will do exactly the same and track a child. You need to show that you are able to demonstrate a clear understanding of your children's needs and meeting the Statutory Framework for the Early Years Foundation Stage.

The dreaded Joint Observation

The inspector will ask the manager to take part in a joint observation throughout the day. The purpose of this is to gather evidence on how well the staff members are engaging with children, and how effectively is the manager able to evaluate the observation and make effective recommendations. It does not necessarily have to be the manager of the setting who takes part with the joint observation, so if you have a teaching and learning member of staff who oversees the overall effectiveness of teaching and learning, they can also observe along with the inspector.

The observation does not necessarily have to written alongside the inspector; however, you do need to share your evaluations of the observation and the differences between the inspector and the observer. The inspector will want to see that you are observing what they are observing and a discussion will be undertaken regarding how to improve on the activity and the staff's interaction with the children.

Joint observations are not able to be carried out with childminders who work alone; however, the inspector will want to observe individual children with the childminder and be able to discuss their learning progress/behaviour. The inspector will observe a specific activity which is planned and discuss about the learning outcomes and how you can improve them. This is a way of evaluating your practice; one important point I want to draw your attention to is that you should not create an activity just for your inspector to see. This has happened many times during my inspections with setting. Not only does it look false, the fact is that children never lie.

Some pointers when creating activities with children: My senior inspector taught me that everything I write as an inspector.

I need to think 'SO WHAT.'
So with that in mind

Firstly, always do activities you know children are interested in. Make a note of their interests as these are ever changing. Another exceptional way is to engage parents with this.

Why not send out this form out to parents every half term so you are able to work in collaboration with them? This shows an excellent working partnership as children's interests maybe different at home to your setting and you will be able to bounce ideas off with each other.

You are also able to choose what activity you wish the inspector to observe with yourself or with your nominated person. If you decide to decline the opportunity; for this to happen, the inspector must record this within her evidence. My recommendation is do not decline this offer. Put this time to good use.

This is your time to shine and think about whether your declining would be a wasted opportunity to show what your setting does, how well your staff interacts with children, the benefits of such activities and the impact it has on the children's development and learning.

So, before the day of the inspection, make sure you have spoken to your staff about what is going to happen on the day and ask your staff if anyone wants to volunteer to be observed. This not only involves all staff members; it also helps them feel valued and a part of the process.

Think about the types of activity you want the inspector to observe and the interactions staff members have with children.

To ensure that you are ready for your inspection, why not start now in measuring how good your teaching/learning/assessment is?

Take the time now before your inspection to address concerns you may have. Ensure that all team members are on board as this will show clarity and consistency when your inspection finally happens. Think about the quality of your staff interactions through their teaching.

Do they understand about sustained shared thinking and are able to question the children to hone those critical thinking skills which are so important in the early stages of a child's life?

Through your own observations monitor the responses of children when being questioned and observe the activities they are participating in.

- Are they encouraging curiosity?
- Are they thinking about investigating further?
- How is communication and language promoted throughout the activities?
- Are staff members making eye contact with children during these valuable conversations and making children feel valued?
- Are they building from children's knowledge, recalling from previous events and using different teaching methods to suit children's learning styles?

I have been to many inspections and observed what it takes to develop an understanding of the observation, assessment and planning cycle. You get this right from today and it is sure to have an infinitely positive impact on children's outcomes and help them prepare better for school.

Use the form below to help you with your Joint observations.

At the end of the joint observation, you and the inspector will discuss your collective findings. Just like with any reflections in your setting, understanding your practice observations is highly important.

They help you and the inspector (and your team) to gain an understanding of the development of your team. It will demonstrate your knowledge on how children are learning and developing and how you as a manager are aware on how to make improvement.

The observations will be able to assess not only practitioners, but also the person who is observing alongside them. They will want to see a good evaluation and how this impacts children and the development of staff members too. This also contributes to the evidence within the sections of teaching, learning and assessment.

If you are part of a childminding network, I would use this opportunity to carry out observations on each other. This shows outstanding practice on how to improve on your own development in a practice where you are very much working on your own.

The inspection handbook (2017) informs us that,

'The inspector and the provider should agree which activities/age groups/care routines to select for the joint observation. After the observation, they should discuss their views about the quality of practice in supporting children's care, learning and development. The inspector should not convey a view about the activity and/or care routine initially but should

ask the provider for their view about its strengths, what would have made it better and how good it was overall.'

If the quality of the practice is not sufficient, it is important that the inspector talks to you about what was observed. The inspector will then want to see what action you are going to take to ensure improvements are made.

You and the inspector will agree on a time to give feedback to the practitioner and manage the situation well.

The inspector may seek the involvement in this scenario, so they are able to see how you as the manager are performing this task.

This is all part of the joint observation and will be recorded within the inspector evidence of the day.

Points to remember:

- Be prepared
- Ensure you are contributing to peer observations before the inspection, so it becomes a natural process within your day to day running
- Be evaluative. Understand what needs to improve and how you are going to achieve this.

Room:			Date:	
Observer 1 name:			Observer 2 name:	
Practitioner being observed:				
Activity being observed:				
Inside/outside (please circle)	Number of children	Focused Activity	Area of provision	Snack or lunch time
Observation:				
Joint Observation Feedback				
Feedback notes from observers				

Feedback from practitioners

Actions Agreed and training required
*

*

*

Signature of Observers :

Signature of practitioners :

Next observation due:

Once you have started using the joint observation format, it will become easier and not be such a shock when you are expected to do this with your inspector. By ensuring that you and your staff members are comfortable with this process, it become natural and this will have an impact on the outcome of your day.

7. PERSONAL DEVELOPMENT, BEHAVIOUR AND WELFARE

During the day of inspection, your inspector will make a judgement on children's personal development, behaviour and welfare. They will do this by evaluating the extent to which you are successfully supporting and promoting the children's well-being.

Inspectors will want to see that children are able to have a sense of achievement of what they are developing in as well as a commitment to learning through the culture of your setting.

Think about how you do that in your setting.

We all know that children need to be able to be confident learners, be very self-aware and understand whether they are successful or not in their achievements of learning. Inspectors will want to see how children bounce back from their less-than-perfect results, if needed, and how they are able to become resilient.

Through life's challenges, children need to be able to bounce back and thrive through the numerous strengths they have achieved. We have an innate drive regarding the capacity of resilience; however, this does have to be worked upon not only in our lives but the lives of children.

We need to be able to encourage resilience with children as early as possible, be the role models that children desire us to be and ensure that we are building and encouraging children's confidence in all levels of their learning and development.

Your inspector will want to see that children are able to be independent and have the ability to explore, think for themselves and use their imagination. Using the basis of Characteristics of Effective Learning will help children prepare for their transitions within your own setting, whether this pertains from room to room or into the reception year at school.

Take the time to reflect upon this in your setting. How do you ensure that children are confident enough to manage these transitions? Write down the transitions your children have and notes with your staff team.

Within these transitions comes emotional security and attachments with practitioners. Attachments with key persons need to be robust to ensure that children are confident within their own development are ready to explore their new surroundings and environment.

Again, take the time to talk to your staff and ask them how extensively they know their key children.
This is so important.
Ask questions such as what the children's likes and dislikes are.

- What are they interested in at present and how is this being developed?
- Are they able to evolve their own learning?
- Do they have a schema and how is this knowledge being used to increase their life skills and improve on their own development?
- Do children feel safe with their peers and show mutual respect?

If questions like these are answered well, you can safely say that your key staff members know their key children and this will be a credit to them.

Key person

Children succeed and thrive from a foundation of secure, warm and loving care provided by the key people in their lives. During the day, we as practitioners become that person by taking on the role of the main carer - providing the stability, support and comfort when children need this. The key person is required to get to know the child's personality well, so that they can understand and meet their needs.

An example of an outstanding personal development, behaviour and welfare report would read like this:

'Children form exceptionally strong emotional bonds with the childminder. They feel extremely secure in the highly welcoming environment where the childminder supports all children to develop excellent levels of independence. For example, she gives young children time and sensitive guidance on going to the toilet. The childminder has an excellent understanding of their moods, feelings and individual personalities, enabling her to support their emotional development extremely successfully. The childminder is particularly very attentive and supervises children exceptionally well. For instance, she explains thoroughly throughout the day about how they can keep themselves safe.'

Catherine Moss, Childminder Farnborough

Think about how you choose the key person for a child.

- Do you wait until a child builds up relationships with an adult when they first start?
- Do you encourage home visits with an allocated key person to meet the child

alongside the parents and start to build on the attachment from the start?

- Or is the key person chosen because they only have seven key children and all the other staff members have eight?

Whichever way you choose the key person, think about the impact this will have on the child. Why are you doing it this way and how can you improve?
We know we can all improve, but ensuring that we are continually striving to develop our own skills, this will guarantee that we are a reflective setting.

With this in mind, do you have a key person policy? Do all staff members know the reason they have been assigned the role of a key person, or is it something you always have done?

Do you have a key person buddy system for when the key person is not in the setting? If so, brilliant, this shows you are ensuring children's needs are being met. If not, introduce this now to ensure you are being consistent.

Why not think about using one as part of your induction programme so that all staff members are aware of the reasons why?

The key person must be able to provide the following for a child:

- Close attachment
- Familiarity

- Supported learning
- Comfort
- Encouragement
- Learning opportunities
- Consistent boundaries

Your inspector will want to see what support each key person gives their key children.

Things to remember:

- How many key children do they have to effectively have a good partnership with the child?
- Does the key person support each of their key children to become familiar with the setting and to feel confident and safe within it?
- Is the key person the practitioner who provides comfort and care for their key child as much as possible?
- Does each key person develop a genuine bond with each child and their parents - supporting children to form secure relationships?

Your inspector will want to see how you promote children's physical and emotional health by monitoring their behaviour and conduct.

Think about how children are able to manage their own feelings and convey this to others. Another useful idea would be is to discuss behaviour at a staff meeting in your setting and work out strategies within your team about how you can improve on this if you have any concerns. Document this as it will show you are being evaluative. Make sure you set a target date of when this needs to be achieved.

Did you know that your local authority will be able to help you with any concerns you may have regarding behaviour? Portage services look at working with families to help them develop and have life experiences for young children.

They are able to support parents, settings and children in minimising barriers that can threaten children and support your services that you can access. Ensuring that you are making accurate observations about children who have concerns with regarding behaviour is principal to ensuring that all outcomes for children are met.

Personal Development

Personal development, behaviour and welfare main evidence will have come from inspector's direct observations of how children behave, and how they interact with staff as well as other children. Inspectors will want to see the quality of care you provide which does includes the routines you are able to secure with babies and young children.

Evidence of planning within the area of children's personal, social and emotional development will be used to see how you are able to supplement the inspector's observations.

The impact of their findings will secure your grading in this area and other pieces of evidence are likely to include:

*   Evidence of how children's well-being is assessed.
*   Discussions with key persons, children and parents regarding the key person system and how effectively this is being used.
*   The inspectors' tracking of children care arrangements, such as the records of accidents, incidents and their attendance - as previously stated.

Attendance

Attendance also needs to be monitored in your setting as this not only ensures the safety of children, but also builds relationships with their own key person. Continuing attendance is so paramount to building relationships with staff and children's peers. The inspector will want to see how you monitor and record attendance.

Do you get parents to sign their children in with a time and signature or do you rely on staff to do this? Whatever way you record this - remember the word impact.
What is the point of you recording this? Remember duty care as well. Regarding attendance records, do

you record the time of arrival and departure of each child? If not, why not?

Exceptional practice in any setting - whether you are full day care or a childminder - is to be able to demonstrate that the need to ensure safety is paramount and high on the agenda of your setting. Recording the time of children arriving and departing with a signature highlight the duty of care you have to protect children. We all know that you have to keep records regarding children for a certain number of years, but think about why we do this.

You have a duty to protect children and show how you are going to achieve this.

You will need to be aware of any patterns of absences that may be suggested to other wider safeguarding concerns. Your inspector will look at how well you work in partnership with parents to promote children's good attendance.

Other pieces of evidence also need to be considered during this area of the inspection in terms of how well your policies and procedures are known by practitioners and how these are evident within your setting.

Are you able to demonstrate this is being cascaded to staff and are they aware of the implications in case of non-compliance?

Behaviour

Within the Statutory Framework for the Early Years Foundation Stage (2017), it is clearly documented

3.52. 'Providers are responsible for managing children's behaviour in an appropriate way. Providers must not give corporal punishment to a child.'

Providers must take all reasonable steps to ensure that corporal punishment is not given by any person who cares for or is in regular contact with a child, or by any person living or working in the premises where care is provided.

Any Early Years provider who fails to meet these requirements commits an offence. Providers, including childminders, must keep a record of any occasion where physical intervention is used, and parents and/or carers must be informed on the same day, or as soon as reasonably practicable.

Writing a behaviour policy is one of the key points in terms of which settings should be following to ensure consistency is adhered to when relaying boundaries with children.

When writing such a policy, it needs to be made clear and concise for all staff members to follow.

You need to ensure that the following points are covered.

- Children need to be able access a caring, positive atmosphere and demonstrate the ability to self-discipline. They need to be kept safe from both physical and emotional harm.

- The expectation of children's behaviour needs to high in embracing honesty and the need for good manners.

- For children to be able to achieve this, there needs to be mutual respect between practitioners and children as well as between staff. The relationships which are maintained need to promote a positive environment and children must have a clear understanding of what acceptable behaviour is/is not.

- Practitioners need to work with parents or carers to help improve the behaviour of children and endeavour to offer a non-confrontational solution when conflicts arise between children and practitioners. This will be provided by inculcating positive attitudes, establishing courtesy towards each other as well as practitioners and reinforcing the importance of parents as role models through being approachable and caring.

- It is a good practice for each setting to have a behaviour management nominated person named within the policy so that practitioners can speak to if they have concerns.

As an example of outstanding practice regarding
Personal development, behaviour and welfare,

**'Children socialise extremely well and have a
wonderful time with their friends. They
demonstrate an exemplary understanding of
sharing. Children thrive on the attention and fun
they have with the childminder. She has an
excellent understanding of their moods, feelings
and individual personalities, enabling her to
support their emotional development extremely
successfully.'**

Nicola Facey, Childminder with assistants, Andover

This section not only covers behaviour management,
but also managing feelings. Your inspector will want
to see how you encourage children to self-regulate
and manage their own feelings throughout the day.
This can be pretty hard to do in everyday situations
and this is where the role of you as practitioners and
knowing your key children is so important.

While your inspector will want to see children
behaving well, this does not mean that they are all
sitting quietly on the table. We all know this is not
possible and not a great way for children to learn and
develop. They need to have the freedom to choose
what they wish and be able to manage their own
feelings with their peers.
We know that some children's behaviour can have a
huge impact on our day itself; can you imagine how

this impacts other children and also the child themselves?

I have grown to love a challenge of behaviour within a setting and find out the root cause of why it is happening. Children's emotional well-being is paramount and holds the key to the success of learning and development. I need you all to be aware when reading this that negative behaviour can be a display of unmet basic needs. You as practitioners will be the first to know the children behaving best through being their key person. Find out why the child is behaving this way and help find a solution. The child is a tiny acorn and will not turn into a proud oak tree without the support of watering and nurturing along its journey.

On occasions, some signs of undesirable behaviour may be a cause for concern and this is abuse (and I am not saying this is true in all cases, but it must be documented and acknowledged). It is your duty of care and part of the reporting requirement for you to recognise signs of any significant changes of behaviour and record/report them, if necessary, following your local areas guidance.

Another reason which may cause unwanted behaviour is that your expectations of what the child can do may be unrealistic for their age and stage of development. This is why it is extremely important for practitioners to have a sound knowledge of child development so as to ensure that their expectations are not too high for children in your setting.

Once practitioners have this knowledge, this then needs to be communicated in a way that the child can understand. It also needs to be consistent. Remember, Rome was not built in a day and a child has taken months to get to this stage of behaviour - so expecting them to change in a week is highly unreasonable and will only make you, your team and the children anxious. Ensure that you keep parents involved in the strategies you have chosen too as your inspector will want to see and hear how effectively you involve all those who are needed to make sure that their needs are being met.

Think about the environment you have enabled children to access.

Points which you may want to consider:

- Is the area too big for children?
- Is there any way you can create quiet spaces for children to take themselves if they need to self-regulate?
- Is there a mixture of children that causes the child to behave in this way?
- Can you create areas and group time which enables the child to learn and develop without becoming angry or anxious which in turn may cause unwanted behaviour?
- Is the space in your setting too visually stimulating?

This is important and some research has shown that the vast array of colours can over stimulate a child's brain and cause behavioural issues. Once any issues of safeguarding concerns have been ruled out and you have ensured that the environment is suitable for a child to learn, the next step would be to identify whether a child needs any additional support through outside agencies. This can impact a child's behaviour as they are not able to comprehend how to calm themselves or communicate effectively. Think about whether a child is having a transition at home which may also have an impact on this; for example, a new baby, divorce of parents, limited language skills, or even the overuse of a digital source such as tablet.

Once every avenue has been thoroughly investigated and researched, only then only can start implementing the strategies which can help children self-regulate. Your inspector will want to see what strategies you have in place for any behavioural issues and how effectively this has helped the child. In addition, use this time to show your observations where you may be able to see what triggers this unwanted behaviour. Make sure you evaluate this and ensure that you explain what you are doing next to help children's behaviour.

How do you include parents/carers, outside agencies, key person and the child in an everyday basis? Your inspector may want to talk to the parents of children you have concerns with to see whether you are sharing this information and they feel happy with the strategies you have in place.

Biting

One common incident in an Early Years setting is biting. This can cause friction between parents and staff, the child who has been bitten and for the biter themselves. This can also quite often be a cause for a complaint.

Think about whether you have a biting policy or is this included in your positive behaviour policy. Your inspector will want to see this policy to make sure that you are following the procedure you claim to follow. This is the purpose of your policies and procedures. What you write in these is what you need to follow!

Do remember that children bite for a reason. Again, you have to find out why. Children do not understand why they feel the need to bite. They do not understand how this can hurt others.

Biting is a form of children being able to explore, especially with young children. Think about whether they are hungry or thirsty as this could perhaps be their way of communicating this to you as they are unable to relay this information any other way.

Some children bite because they are teething or because they want your attention. If this is the case, turn your attention to the child who has been bitten as they need it more at that time. Children who have communication and language difficulties sometimes bite to get themselves heard.

I know I hear you say they are certainly doing that. If this is happening, think about outside agencies that can help you with encouraging children to communicate, such as visual cards or sign language. One setting I had visited in my travels had a time out area where children went to sit on and learn to 'calm down' when displaying unwanted behaviour.

It got to the point where children took themselves to this place in order to calm down. Think about the impact this has on the child in this area. Is this really an appropriate strategy to use to help children to display positive behaviour! I am hoping you are saying it isn't!

The word SORRY!

There has been much debate about encouraging young children to say sorry. According to common notion, this could have the opposite effect of what you are trying to achieve and will lead children to not developing a proper understanding and becoming less kind and caring.

This is hard as we are brought up in a nation of saying sorry for just the simplest of things. Think about it - as nation do we say sorry for the slightest of things and does this really make us feel sorry? Try and encourage children to realise what they have done when they have displayed this behaviour and how it makes the other child/person feel.

As a practitioner, talk to the child who is the victim and explain to them that you are sorry that another child has hurt them as this turns your attention away from the perpetrator and turn your focus to the other child. This will encourage children to develop empathy skills; eventually, the child will start to display how sorry they really are.

If this is the way you encourage children in your setting, make sure you put this in your positive behaviour policy and explain the reason to the inspector. They will want to know the impact of your decision in your setting. Again, the word IMPACT comes into play.

You need to provide clear guidance to your inspector for what the children's understand of being acceptable behaviour is, and if you have older children; for example, in an afterschool club it is a good idea to encourage children to create their own behaviour contract.

I have seen this in several afterschool clubs. Not only does it give older children a sense of autonomy, it also gives them a sense of self-worth that they are being listened to. When your inspector arrives in your afterschool setting, encourage children to talk to the inspector and explain about how they put the contract and rules together. This is highly effective and also covers British Values given that children have a voice and are able to give opinions.

Welfare

How are children keeping themselves safe? does this include the use of the internet and social media?

This may not be suitable for your Early Years setting, but if you are a childminder or afterschool club, how do you ensure children are keeping themselves safe and what documentation and safety measures do you have in place to protect children?

Fundamental British Values

Under this area, children's personal development will be monitored, thinking about how well prepared they are in the context of a wider society and life in Britain. This means that fundamental British values will need to be evidenced to show its impact on children. This, however, does not mean a display board. This is not what your inspector wants to see. They will want to see how children are able to understand the rules within your setting. Are they involved in making these rules?

I have seen many settings who are able to exemplify British values in their everyday practice and here are just some examples.

Rule of Law

Children in an afterschool club are able to create their own rules. They use this time to discuss what they want to follow in their setting and create a poster to remind all children that the rules were *made by children, for children.* The impact was huge as it gave children the autonomy and self-confidence and self-worth helping boost their self-esteem.

A preschool I visited a few years ago used super hero characters as their rules. For example, at a child's height, they had placed several of these as reminders to themselves of what is right or wrong. Superman was used as a reminder to use their walking feet. Similarly, Snow White was a reminder to be polite by saying please and thank you, wherever Spiderman was used to be kind with our hands.

I observed children reminding others of these characters. For example, when running, one child pointed his friend to Superman and recapped the need to walk. This was a delight to see and is a great example of the rules made by children for children ethos.

Mutual respect and tolerance

Mutual respect and tolerance for others is about learning to understand and appreciate each other's differences without allowing those differences to cause a change in treatment of any sort. It is about being a cohesive part of a community where not everyone is the same and forming relationships within that without discrimination.

Think about how you promote this in your setting. Naturally, we are promoting inclusivity where we value different faiths and cultures, but how do we explore these fully to ensure that we are encouraging that children to recognise differences and similarities and are able to share what we know with each other.

Again, your inspector does not want to see the obligatory display board with people all around the world. Think about what impact this has on children's learning. Think about every day practice and how you encourage children to tolerate each other. Children need to be given a wide range of opportunities to be able to practice tolerance and challenge any stereotypical behaviour they may occur. Children also need to be able to share ideas and stories that really value their diverse experiences and encourage them to learn from each other.

Individual Liberty

As well as children being confident learning who are self-aware, they need to have a positive sense of themselves. You can provide opportunities for children to develop this and increase their confidence in their own abilities. Enable children to have a voice and take risks, talk about their own experiences, explore own feelings, reflect on their differences and value other children's opinions as well.

Having the chance to share how they are feeling when they are preparing for transition to school is one observation I was able to make in a pre-school I inspected. They used the small group time to prepare children for their next stage of their learning; they were able to listen and used the loose parts table for children to illustrate how they were feeling by looking in a mirror and creating their emotions on the wood slice.

Practitioners were able to talk to children about what they would be feeling when they started Year R. In fact, they did not call it 'Big School' as they felt this would create anxiety among children and wanted to encourage their confidence for the next stage of their lives. The impact was indeed thought provoking within this setting as children were given a voice and were being heard. They relished in their key person engaging in conversation with them, and you could see that children were very confident and excited about the next phase of their journey.

Democracy

As part of democracy in British Values, children need to be able to have a vote. This links to personal, social and emotional development and practitioners need to encourage children to know their views count, value each other's views and make decisions as a collective force. An idea would be to encourage children to vote on what the activity they liked best during the day. Children should be given adequate opportunities to develop their curious minds where their questions are being valued.

This area of the Common Inspection Framework is of highest importance. We truly want children to achieve in all areas of teaching, learning and assessment, but can they really do this significantly if they are not achieving in PDBW?

There have been three occasions where I have given an *outstanding* grade to settings for this area and *good* for all other areas. I believe that children's emotional well-being does affect their behaviour and welfare. Get this right and children will be in the right place for them to learn effectively. This is so important. We sometimes forget that children have feelings and the things we do to ensure they are learning can be reduced to a tick box exercise.

Take this time to reflect on your setting and think about the last time you spent time just listening to a child's conversation, their worries and successes without ensuring you have recorded it somewhere.

Keeping children healthy

Ask yourself and your staff on how they and the children keep themselves healthy. This is a good staff meeting exercise as when asked this question by the inspector, practitioners can often freeze and struggle to explain themselves without getting flustered. Part of the reporting requirements is to explain to your inspector about how you keep children physically active. Do your staff members know how many minutes of the day children need to be active?

With 1 in 10 children not meeting the minimum required amount of being physically active each day, the Department of Health campaign aims for children to be moving and promoting physical activity for at least 180 minutes per day. This can be recognised as tummy play in babies to being able to walk unaided as they grow from toddlers to children at the age of 5 as not sitting for long periods of time.

There have been many settings I have visited where they have taken away the chairs and used small quiet spaces for children to use when they need to rest. This impact shows that children are active when they are standing at a table doing an activity. Take this time to reflect upon how much sitting down a child does in your setting and how can you show that you are encouraging them to be physically active.

There has been much discussion regarding the amount of time children are engaged in screen time and how settings are not adequately making sure their environment is challenging enough for them. Children need to be able to make choices, but these need to be healthy choices.

Think about the snacks children are able to have.

Do children have a choice and is the choice wide-ranging? Do you speak to children about healthy food and encourage this from an early age?

One setting I visited created a lovely activity at their 'coming together' time, often called circle time.

Children were asked to sit down a circle and there were two trays and a basket of snacks in the middle. I, along with the manager of the setting, was observing this activity.

The purpose was - is the snack a want or a need?

Lots of thought provoking questioning was used to extend children's understanding on why we need certain foods. Children delighted in sharing how it would make them big and strong. Practitioners explained the difference between a want and a need to the children.
Children encouraged each other and shared their points of view of about the want for a biscuit - but the need for a banana.

Personal self-help skills

Encouraging children to be healthy is high on the Ofsted agenda and you will need to be able to demonstrate this to your inspector. Think about how you support children to be independent throughout their time with you in your setting.

There are many ways you can do this - from toileting to encouraging children to wash their hands to even the simplest of things such as blowing nose.

- If you see a child who needs their nose wiped, what do you do?
- Do you get a tissue and wipe their nose for them?

- Do you ask them to find the tissue box and collect a tissue?
- Or do you have a nose blowing station where children are able to do this for themselves and see what they are doing?

I have seen this in several settings now and highly recommend it being in place in all rooms from the toddlers to preschool.

Set aside and area where there is an acrylic mirror on the walk with words to the effect of *does your nose need blowing* to be in place to be part of rich print areas for children to see clearly. In addition, a mirror is placed on a table that has a box of tissues which are replenished as soon as they are finished, along with a bowl of soapy water and hand towels. Encourage children to look in the mirror and explain to them about keeping their noses clean and washing their hands after doing so.

One setting I visited were concerned that children were using the same water to wash their hands. I would recommend the water to get changed every few hours, but there is nowhere in the Statutory framework which states that this is unhealthy.

Children acquire a strong sense of emotional well-being. They are great risk assessors and show self-control in a range of situations. For example, when being builders children are aware of the need to wear safety goggles. Children have access to a wealth of interesting and innovative resources and play experiences that greatly support their interests. For example, children use magnets to investigate which objects are metal and they share their findings with others. Children relish their time as the 'responsible' helper. They confidently take orders from their friends and help to serve them healthy snacks.

Compton and Shawford Preschool

This is an excellent way of encouraging children to be independent with their self-help skills. You must make sure that you have the following as part of the welfare requirements

'Where food and snacks and drinks are provided they must be healthy, balanced and nutritious' – How do you ensure what you provide comprises of all these things?

Think about children's lunchboxes; how do you ensure these are healthy?

When parents visit with their child at the very beginning, now is the time to actually talk about what is expected from parents, especially in the lunch boxes. Talk about how there may be allergies within the setting and you need to make sure that children are kept safe from any unwanted goodies (which is a want, not a need) such as crisps, chocolate and sweets.

Fresh drinking water must be available at all times – How do you do this? Please be mindful that if children have their own drink bottles, they only access this as opposed to just taking any random bottle at any time. Stomach bugs can become widespread all too quickly and this needs to be monitored constantly.

There must be an area which is adequately equipped to provide healthy snacks and drinks. Include suitable hygienic preparation of food and drink for children.

How do you ensure that the areas where you prepare bottles and food are constantly cleaned? Do you document this?

These are only just a handful of the welfare requirements which need to be abided by. See the Statutory requirements of the Early Years Foundation Stage for the full version.

The childminder's home is exceptionally well prepared to help children develop their self- help skills. She has designed the play areas to support children extremely effectively. For example, the den with storybooks provides a communication-friendly space. The space under the table supports social skills and she provides small spaces for the children to be comfy and secure. This helps children to choose where they need to play to meet their own needs. Toddlers are learning the impact of their behaviour on others. For example, when children are playing on and near the slide they think about how to share the space safely. Children thoroughly enjoy their meals and have a very sociable time.

**Lynda Hall,
Childminder
Tadley**

One final point to make in this section is:
How do you ensure that children know about similarities and differences between themselves and others and among families, faiths, communities, cultures and traditions?

When I asked these questions during my Quality Improvement visits as well as early years inspections, I often heard the reply, 'well we have a Polish little boy and we ask his parents for words to help him understand and we invite them in to talk to the children.' Another classic example is, 'we celebrate Chinese New Year and do food tasting.'

No disrespect to these activities which you are providing for the children, but think about when a child leaves your setting. What cultures are they are able to see and relate to? Are they able to see any cultures or faiths? Ensure that you are able to demonstrate to your inspector that you are encouraging children to be aware of the cultures and faiths of other children's and their families.

This all comes under the umbrella of mutual respect and tolerance, and should be able to be demonstrated in your setting. Think about the kind of impact this has on children's lives and how we can start encouraging children to be asking questions about how other people live from all around the world.

8. OUTCOMES FOR CHILDREN

The final reporting judgement is *Outcomes for children.*

This can also be linked well with teaching, learning and assessment as it is essentially about how children are progressing and being prepared for their next stage of learning and whether this is the next room in your setting or entering school.

This area of your inspection will take into account the current levels of progress and development that the children are making. Your inspector will make a judgement using the grade descriptors on the learning outcomes which children are achieving and evaluate the following.

- How are children progressing in their starting points?
- How are children meeting or exceeding the level of development that is typical for their age?

- Are they are able to move onto the next stage of their learning

The way an inspector can collate this evidence should come from a direct observation of children's learning and their outcomes. This will then need to be demonstrated in the way in which you assess this information. This will also be the way you have assessed children and documented this – and whether this is an accurate document.

Your inspector will want to see where children are when they start with you.

So let's think about how you do this in your setting.

How soon after a child starts with you do you start to assess them? Why do you wait this long and what impact does this have? This ranges in every setting which I have inspected in and I always ask the question - why do you wait this long?

This is called baseline assessments. Some settings I have visited encourage parents to assess their children when they start and use this as a basis for starting points. Firstly, as much as this is a great start to work with parents, can you honestly say that parents are able to assess their children correctly and that children do not behave differently at home than they do in a setting? (See also Teaching, Learning and Assessment chapter)

mmendation would be to let the child settle
tart the baseline in all areas around the 2-3
week mark, depending on how often they attend your
setting; obviously, the more they attend, the more
secure they should be feeling. In effect, the
assessment process will be more effective.

Another recommendation I have which is also very
effective and one that I take into every quality
improvement inspection is this: when a child moves
from room to room, do a baseline assessment after 2-
3 weeks again covering all areas.

This will ensure consistency in the assessments and
any areas which need further development can be
actioned immediately. In turn, this helps reduce the
differences between each child and cohort. This will
also ensure there are no gaps and that the children's
developmental needs are met from day one.

Children need to meet or exceed their level of
development that is typical for their right age, so that
they can move onto the next stage of their learning.

*'Children engage energetically in their investigations. While
playing with toy animals, they discover that, just like us, there
can be mummy, daddy and baby animals. They arrange these
into family groups while others look on a map at where they
live. Children are actively involved in communicating with
children in different countries. For example, using technology,
they recently experienced the festival of paper in Japan. Children
wrote wishes and sent copies to each other. They placed the*

wishes on bamboo trees alongside the ones sent to them, setting fire to release them in England and Japan, together.'

Yorley Barn Nursery
School, Sudbury, Suffolk

The Early Years Inspection Handbook (2017) states: *'Any evaluation of children's progress towards the early learning goals must be judged in relation to their starting points, their individual needs, how long they have been at the provision and how often they attend. The inspector should examine the information that the provision gathers about what children know, can do and enjoy when they start to attend.'*

- So when a child starts with you, what do you do to gather all the right information?
- Do parents and key people complete *all about me* form which has details on to explain the interests of the child?
- Do you encourage parents to highlight where they think a child is in their stage of learning?
- If so, how do you do this and what IMPACT does it have on children's outcomes?

Your inspector will want to see any evidence gathered from children's starting points and this can also be gained by talking to both practitioners and parents about the level of children's social, communication and physical skills upon entering the setting and how these are observed when they are new into the setting.

The inspector will use this evidence to evaluate how well you know about, and understand the progress children are making towards the early learning goals. The inspector must judge whether the adults' expectations for children are high enough whilst also seeing how confident you are in children's development.

In addition, the inspector will want to see children who are disadvantaged and those who are under-achieving or are catching up quickly. How do you monitor and ensure this is happening? You will also need to demonstrate how a child at the age of two is using the Progress check at 2 form.

How to ensure that his is being assessed and written correctly?

The Early Years Foundation Stage (EYFS, 2017) requires that parents and carers must be supplied with a short written summary of their child's development in the three prime learning and development areas of the EYFS:

- ✓ Personal, Social and Emotional Development
- ✓ Physical Development
- ✓ Communication and Language

This happens ideally around 2 years 4 months and its purpose is to support practitioners, parents as well as other outside agencies to see where a child is and enable an early identification of any developmental needs, so that additional support maybe sought.

You need to remember that there is no particular format which needs to be recorded, but the only information which needs to be provided is the prime areas.

The aims of the progress check are to:

- Enable you as a practitioner to understand a child's needs and plan for them effectively
- Review a child's in the three prime areas only

- Provide parents with a clear understanding of their child's stage of development

- Enable parents to support children at home to enhance their learning

- Provide actions of what you intend to do in order to ensure the children are meeting their milestones and what support you give to them

The Progress Check at 2 should be completed by the key person who should know the child really well. They must use their observations in the setting to see which stage the child's knowledge is in, how they understand what they are learning and their behaviour - whilst also considering the views of parents as well as other practitioners such as the inclusion office, if necessary, in the setting.

You will need to explain to the inspector what you do with this information and who you give this to.

So, think about this information.

Who do you give the report to? Is it just to the parents or carers of the child? If it is, why do you only give this to them?

Every child has a health visitor who also completes a check at 2 which is recorded. What impact would it have if you sent a copy of the progress at 2 not only to parents but also to the Health visitor? This is an excellent way of demonstrating how well you work in partnership with others and would serve as a great example of explaining to your inspector that you are proactive enough to work with others at all times in order to meet the needs of children.

If you have any children that have special educational needs or any disabilities, you need to be able to demonstrate how you are supporting the progress of these children. This is, again, a very important point. All outcomes need to be consistent in all areas and if not, you will need to explain why not and what/how you are intending to improve upon these.

Children who speak English as an additional language need to be able to gain the skills they need to communicate effectively. Again, think about how you do this in your setting.

Your inspector will make an evaluation of children's outcomes and should take account of the proportions of children who have made typical progress (or more) from their starting points. An example of typical progress for a child would be that they consistently display the knowledge, skills and understanding that are typical for their age. They would also be moving steadily towards the early learning goals; you are able to show this using your knowledge and assessments of those children.

Children who commence at a lower level of development than is typical for their age should be seen to be able to catch up and make steady progress quickly. A child joining the setting at a higher level of development than would be typical must be given challenges to deepen their learning; this is so important.

Every child needs to be focused on by their key person - and assessments, observations and activities need to be able to show that you are meeting every child's needs.

Overall quality and effectiveness of your provision

Your inspector will want to be able to see the following, and it is up to you to ensure that they are able to see this by being consistent, transparent and clear in your delivering of early years.

Inspectors will evaluate and report on:

- How well your setting meets the needs of the range of children who attend

- The contribution of your setting to children's well-being

- The quality of leadership and management of your setting.

Inspectors will also take into account of all the judgements made across the evaluation schedule. They will also need to consider:

- The progress all children make in their learning and development relative to their starting points as well as their readiness for the next stage of their education.

- The extent to which the learning and care provided by the setting meets the needs of the range of children who attend, including the needs of any children who have special educational needs and/or disabilities

- Children's personal and emotional development, including whether they feel safe and are secure and happy

- Whether the requirements for children's safeguarding and welfare have been fully met and there is a shared understanding/responsibility of how to protect children

- The effectiveness of leadership and management in evaluating practice and securing continuous improvement that improves children's life chances.

Here is a lovely example from an outstanding report for Outcomes for children.

'Children develop excellent skills and are ready to move on to their next stage of learning. They develop outstanding number skills and they practise simple sums while counting their favourite toys and items. Children develop extremely good language and they sing songs and chat as they play alongside each other, for example, at the play dough table. Children are extremely independent, confident and really enjoy learning, paving the way successfully for their move to school.'

**Maimuna Khan,
childminder**

So, with the final chapter on the inspection process now completed... With all this information which is now spinning in your head... What do you do now?

9. SO WHAT NOW?

So, you have taken the time to read the book, dipped into each chapter to explore what you need to do to be prepared for your inspection, but what do you do next, WHAT NOW?

I am hoping you will have made notes along the way as an action plan of what you are planning to improve upon. This is an excellent way of reflecting on your practice as well as showing your inspector how you are evaluating as this is still a reporting requirement.

There may still be times when you are thinking what else can I do? I need an outsider to come in with a fresh pair of eyes to see it for themselves.

This is where Jigsaw Early Years Consultancy comes into its own.

You have read the background and the WHY of us at the very beginning of this book. If this is something you feel you may benefit from then give us a ring, or email or even message.

Our website is www.jigsawearlyyearsconsultancy.com
Our facebook page is:
https://www.facebook.com/JigsawEYC/
Facebook group: Ask to join JigsawEYC
Instagram: Jigsaw_EYC

I thought I would leave you with a few testimonials from settings who have used our Quality Improvement Inspections as part of their evaluation.

Dear Vanessa,

Thank you very much for your visit to our nursery for a Quality Improvement Inspection. As a twice 'Outstanding' nursery, who work incredibly hard to maintain that standard all of the time, we really wanted to be ready, to be confident and as well prepared for our big day as we could be to put us in the best possible position to maintain our grading, so felt that a QII would be exactly what we needed. You were recommended to us by a trusted colleague, and now we recommend you in turn.

Your visit was inspiring; you were professional and courteous, thorough and that filled us with confidence in your feedback. Staff were given valuable experience of inspection and were left feeling more confident, and even excited for their opportunity to shine. Your managers interview and paperwork review was thorough and found a few issues that we have been able to rectify before they cost us our Outstanding, which was exactly what we wanted.

We have already booked you to come and give our new nursery a QII, as well as some consultancy on how to develop that new team, and I am excited and confident about our future, knowing that I have your input and support behind me and my team.

Thank you very, very much again for such a positive experience.

With kindest regards,

Charlotte de Lacey
The de Lacey Montessori School & The de Lacey Day Nursery School.

Background to visit. After a very disappointing Oftsed visit, the Early Years at our school needed a thorough rethink. I was made Early Years Lead in February and began to analyse how the department could be improved. My own personal remit was to make it an 'outstanding' provider.

I had already started to implement changes but the enormity of what I had taken on was beginning to become apparent. Endless nights of trawling through Government requirements, joining chat groups for Early Years practitioners, visiting other provided... I needed help, support and guidance.

Late one night, I came across a competition for a QII and entered. Blow me down, a week later I received an email to explain that I had won! I never win anything. Thinking this could possibly be some kind of hoax, I phoned Vanessa at Jigsaw Consultancy. It wasn't a hoax. She really wanted to help. Vanessa listened to the background of the setting and wanted as much information as possible before her visit.

On the day of the visit, Vanessa arrived and immediately I could see her quietly assessing every aspect of the department. She spoke to staff in what appeared to be a very informal manner, but she was consistently acquiring an overview of the areas that needed to be addressed. As we talked throughout the morning I made notes of her recommendations (5 pages!). However, at the end of our meeting Vanessa bought up every single point I had noted and also made more suggestions.

I had been 'Jigsawed'! I had a list the length of my arm. However, Vanessa followed up her visit with friendly emails to ensure that I was dealing with issues in a systematic and achievable way.

I have recently written a list of changes that have been implemented following her visit and I could now see that the department had changed and was moving forward in the right direction. There is still a lot more work to do, but Vanessa helped to shape these changes in a manageable way.

We are due a monitoring visit from Ofsted and also Vanessa is coming back to help some more! I will update you on the future outcomes for our Early Years Department.

P.S. Vanessa is now known as my Fairy Godmother

So, here's the update I promised!

Since the beginning of May I have been waking up every morning thinking 'today's the day'. The six months from our inspection had passed. The changes needed to meet standards had been met or were being addressed. We were ready for a visit. I truly wanted it to happen before the summer holidays, so the team could have a well-earned rest.

Vanessa came back on the Monday 2ⁿᵈ July 2018. She was blown away by the changes that had taken place. The setting was vibrant, energetic and full of happy children and staff. She agreed that we were ready for a visitor from HMI. There were 3 days left until the end-of-term. Surely they wouldn't come now?

Wednesday 3ʳᵈ July... All of the children were registered and had begun their last full day of planned learning. I looked at the clock, 9:35am. I had lost hope that we'd be inspected before the summer break.
Then the Deputy Head popped her head into the room and looked at me with huge eyes, "Ofsted are here!" Behind me was a scene of devastation. The children had had a lot of fun that morning.

My TA and I looked at each other. Without saying a word to each other we knew what to do! Carry on and just do what we would normally do. I asked the children to put their wiggly fingers to work and tidy up. It was as if they could tell that they needed to do their best. Each child went off and completed a little task. One little boy looked at me and said "We're doing a good job just for you". (A goose bump moment mixed with a slight feeling nausea)

As the inspector arrived in the Early Years block I was in the middle of my phonics session. The children were on form! We had laughing and the children knew all their first three sets of sounds.

Somehow during all of this I had managed to find the time to phone Vanessa. The inspector wanted to speak to her too!

I was asked to attend an interview at 12:30pm with the inspector. It was a grilling, but I survived with support from my Deputy and Head also present. I started waffling about my passion for the department. Then verbal diarrhea kicked in! He wanted me to supply him with some pieces of evidence to back up my claims. I ran off and returned them to him. He was on his own in the office. He thanked me and said with a wry smile "I think what I'm seeing here is rather good".
At the end of the day the Head called us all together and said that although she was not legally able to divulge the outcome of the inspection, she wanted us all to go home and have a well-earned rest with maybe a few glasses of bubbles.

Now, the long wait over the summer holidays for the report and findings to be audited. Watch this space for the next update. Another HUGE thank you to Vanessa. We couldn't have got to this point without your help.

Early years setting, West Sussex

First of all, sorry for the long post - but it's the truth (I haven't been bribed into anything - it's from the heart)
I can't recommend Jigsaw Training enough. I do owe a lot to Vanessa. Thanks to her awesome training and signposting I managed to achieve "Outstanding" in my inspection last week. I was really craving an outstanding grade this time, as previously had 2 "Good" inspections.

The first training I attended was "Safeguarding" run on a Saturday. It was affordable and the location was perfect. Having enjoyed the training and the way Vanessa makes quite serious topics interesting and engaging - I booked onto another training session in Gosport for Characteristics of Effective Learning, British Values and Everyday Maths. CoEL and British Values were topics I just couldn't get my head round.

Having attended the training all was crystal clear and I implemented these "new found" topics into my practice. It was at this particular training that something stuck with me. The talk was about having a "Good" grade and how far and wide this grade can be but why not aim for an "outstanding". Those words just stuck with me. Why not?

Another training I attended was a Webinar on "Are you ready?" - this was also very helpful when I had the call from the inspector. I remained calm and asked all the questions I wanted to prior to her arriving. I would recommend this particular training especially if you are due an inspection, all you really need is covered within this topic.

No doubt I have booked onto Autumn training too which the OI was happy to see in my CPD folder.

Its affordable, informative, fun and full of passion - not a moment to be bored whether it be something important like Safeguarding or something fun like Everyday Maths. Thanks #jigsawconsultancy #awesometraining #youarethesource #SoWhat

**Maimuna Khan,
childminder,
Hampshire**

Vanessa spent a full day at our nursery and I can honestly say it was the most interesting, beneficial experience we have ever had. Vanessa has to be one of the most knowledgeable and experienced professionals within the early year's sector I have ever met. She simply oozes with passion and to quote Vanessa herself, she very definitely has 'fire in her belly' for everything early years.

We gained so much from Vanessa's visit, she gave us lots of useful pointers and ideas to enable us to further improve some areas of our practice. Most importantly for us though, she boosted our confidence in the work that we have been doing surrounding loose parts and evolving our learning environments to continue to inspire our children's natural curiosity.

Thank you so much Vanessa, spending a day in your company was for all of us truly inspiring.

**Jane Broughton, Manager of Tinkerbells
Bridgeinn Day Nursery, Preston, Lancashire**

Well I would like to thank Vanessa for her inspiration!! She helped us with our Quality Improvement inspection giving us the vision to bring our 2 settings together!

And with this we have received an **outstanding** *grade - yes we smashed it!!*

I cannot recommend Vanessa enough!! Let's her see your environment with a fresh pair of eyes - a new perceptive! Cheers

Wendy Hamley, Manager of Courtmoor playschool, Fleet

Final words

I did not intend to use this book to help promote Jigsaw Quality Improvement Inspections but to help you in your upcoming Ofsted inspections. I often have said during the writing of this. *I wish I had this book when I was due an inspection!*

If this is what you are saying then my mission is done. I want you to shine in your inspection and showcase your setting. It is your one and only chance and if I can help you with that at all I have succeeded in my mission!

Printed in Great Britain
by Amazon